SO-AAZ-302

For
CHRIS THOMPSON
whose generous friendship and
support is greatly appreciated.

ART OF THE
NINJA

Peter Lewis

GALLERY BOOKS
An Imprint of W. H. Smith Publishers Inc.
112 Madison Avenue
New York City 10016

Concept, design and editorial by
Mackenzie Publishing Limited,
178 Royal College Street, London NW1 0PS
Great Britain

Editorial: **Jeff Groman**
Design, Art Direction and Production: **Terry Allen**
Design Assistant: **Christine Nys**
Project Co-Ordinator: **Christina Grant**

© Mackenzie Publishing Limited/Peter Lewis 1988

First published in Great Britain in 1988 by
Ward Lock Limited, 8 Clifford Street,
London W1X 1RB, an Egmont Company

This edition published by Gallery Books, an
imprint of W.H. Smith Publishers Inc.,
112 Madison Avenue, New York, New York 10016

ISBN 0-8317-0477-2

Printed in Hong Kong by Regent Publishing
Services Ltd.

CONTENTS

INTRODUCTION

Elite fighting units have existed in practically every civilization since the dawn of time. The Romans had their Praetorian Guard, the ancient Greeks their army of Spartans. Throughout history specialist groups have been established for the sole purpose of their expertise in weaponry and waging war to win at any cost.

Quite often these small groups were successful where huge armies were not. Highly-trained personnel, honed to perfection through intensive specialist training, can — and have — wreaked havoc by infiltrating unseen behind enemy lines to ply their trade with devastating results. Even in the modern era of warfare, governments have initiated the forming of such elite brigades to tactically strike at the very heart of the enemy's bosom, and such groups as the US Delta Force and Great Britain's Special Air Service carry on the traditions of espionage and covert activities.

A special breed

In all of these specialist units, past and present, the common factor was that they were all a very special breed of men — men in peak physical condition, experts in their chosen field, and absolutely committed in their endeavours. But in each case, these men were recruited from an existing army, and then selected for specialist training. In a few short months an intensive and gruelling training regimen produced a combat-ready soldier who, in terms of expertise, was far in advance of the ordinary infantryman. If one could take that intensive training a quantum leap forwards, and extend the few months into 18 years or so, the end product would probably be little short of a superman — a warrior whose skills both mentally and physically would be truly awesome.

Such a unit does in fact exist, and its elite warrior traditions stretch back in time more than a thousand years. They are the ninja, the practitioners of the art of ninjutsu.

Deadliest fighting machine

No fighting unit has captured the imagination in recent years more so than Japan's legendary ninjas. The ninja has often been described as the deadliest fighting machine in the history of warfare. These black-garbed warriors swept through the pages of Japan's turbulent history leaving a trail of mayhem and death in their wake. Totally without morals these assassins of the night killed without fear or favour, hiring themselves out to the highest bidder.

Trained from birth, the ninja's only aim was completely to master techniques of espionage, weapons, unarmed combat, poisons and psychology. These skills were necessary in order that the ninja could facilitate information through their clandestine activities and report to their superiors everything they had learned.

At their height the ninja and their black arts flourished for over 600 years — until the coming of modernization. Then the ninja clans, as they were known, disbanded. Some were lost forever, but a few gained employment either with government agencies or on the other side of the law in the pay of the Japanese criminal organizations known as 'Yakuza'. Thus in a perverted sense they kept alive the traditions and practices of the black assassins.

The ninja live on

With the advent of the popular martial arts in the 1970s, ninjutsu shed its cloak of past infamy and established itself as a respectable martial discipline. The popularity of ninjutsu took off at an astonishing rate worldwide. Spurred on by media promotions, such as TV, video and the movies, the assassins' art emerged into the eighties as a fighting art *par excellence*. An art whereby its adepts could train not only in unarmed combat and weaponry, but also adopt principles of ninja philosophy as a guide for living life and facing day-to-day trials and tribulations with impunity.

Left: *The ninja art of **goton-po**, that of blending in with the environment. The ninja field agent only ever fought an enemy as a last resort, preferring anonymity to discovery.*

Following page: *The ninja's covert activities often entailed travelling through water. Their body movements had to be so subtle that neither a ripple or splash could be detected by the enemy and thus alert the ever-watchful samurai sentries.*

1

BORN OF BLOOD-NINJA HISTORY

Arouse a bee, and it will come at you with the force of a dragon

The exact origins of the ninja and their art of ninjutsu are shrouded in ancient myths. Legends abound as to their early beginnings, some believing they were the descendants of 'Tengu', the devil bird of Japanese mythology. Most historians generally accept that ninjutsu was founded through political and religious upheaval in a period around the end of the sixth century AD in Japan. However, although the first ninja clans established themselves in Japan, it is to China we must look for their origin.

The Art of War
In China during the period known as the Warring States, around 500 BC, a great Chinese general and military strategist named Sun Tsu wrote a book on warfare called *The Art of War*, which was a treatise on the exact science of subjects such as offensive strategy, weakness and strengths of the enemy, terrain, employment of spies, guerrilla warfare, and vulnerability. This book was regarded as standard reading for Chinese intellectuals and military men and even the Taoist and Buddhist priests were well acquainted with its contents.

Sun Tsu was well aware that combat involved a great deal more than just a collision of armed men. Mere numbers alone, he stated in *The Art of War*, conferred no advantage. For a military man living in an age of constant violence, Sun Tsu had an extraordinary air of peace and tranquillity about him. He did not conceive war in terms of slaughter and destruction, but believed an objective should and could be taken with the proper use of strategy and sound

information of the enemy's plans. His prime directive was that 'the skilful strategist should be able to subdue the enemy's army without engaging it, take his cities without laying siege to them, and overthrow his State without bloodying swords'. He always cautioned his emperor not to place reliance on sheer military power. Being a staunch advocate of espionage and covert operations he counselled that to use his tactics would contribute to a speedy outcome of an impending war. This highly informative book upon waging war, being well known to the wandering priests of the time, was instrumental in the birth of what was soon to be known as ninjutsu.

Forest demons
In the vast woodlands of northern China, bands of robbers existed in great numbers. One of these robber groups lived in the very heart of the forest. The priests on their many travels often sought refuge and shelter for the night with these bands of brigands, who were called by the simple Chinese peasants *lin kui* or forest demons. The *lin kui* had learned to survive with nature in harmony and everything they needed to live was gleaned from the vast forests. Food, shelter, clothes, all were obtained from their natural habitat. They only ventured into the then civilized world to earn money either by robbing or hiring themselves out to local warlords to spy on possible enemies. It would seem only natural then that over the years the travelling priests picked up much information of how these *lin kui* lived and survived. This knowledge was to come in use at a later date.

Severe internal problems within China, fuelled by

political intrigue around the emperor's court, led to many revolts, that were always put down with much bloodshed. Scholars and priests alike fell from royal favour and patronage at the Sui dynasty (AD 589-618) court. Consequently many intellectuals had to flee their homeland and seek sanctuary in the islands of Japan. They took with them all the knowledge that they had accumulated over the centuries.

First espionage agents

Upon arrival in their new land the dissidents, especially the priests, settled in remote mountainous areas around the provinces of Iga and Koga, little knowing that they were soon to be disturbed by events that were taking place in the Japanese political arena.

The Prince Regent of Japan at that time was Shotoku, a fervent Buddhist who was engaged in a battle for succession to the throne against a usurper named Moriya. Shotoku, on the advice of the Buddhist priests who had gained access to the royal Japanese court through religious influence, engaged men to spy and gather information on his rival. This was the first authenticated account of espionage agents ever being used in Japan.

When Shotoku finally became ruler he promulgated Buddhism above all other religions and for a time Japan's own indigenous religion of Shinto had to take a back seat. For 30 years Buddhism flourished under Shotoku until his death in AD 622.

Then the various religious factions became embroiled in a bloodthirsty power struggle over which doctrine should be designated as the state religion. The struggle soon got out of hand and began to involve everybody. Such was the disorder, that the country began to suffer great stress both governmentally and economically. However, a man came forward in the guise of a saviour. He was En-no-Gyoja, a mountain warrior ascetic or priest that the Japanese people called *yamabushi* (warrior priest). Trying to solve the dispute and restore order he promoted a different form of Buddhism called Shugendo. This new religion quickly gained much support from the people and became very popular. However, it was inevitable that the court aristocracy and the rich landowners would fear that En-no-Gyoja and his followers were gaining too much power. They had to be stopped before the scruffy *yamabushi* had ideas upon the throne itself. To force a showdown the various petty officials mustered a huge army and sent them out to defeat En-no-Gyoja.

Mountain stronghold of the yamabushi

Greatly outnumbered the *yamabushi* were slaughtered in their hundreds. The few that remained beat a hasty retreat to the vast and remote mountainous regions of Iga on the island of Honshu in central Japan to lick their wounds. This desolate area was shrouded in mists, the mountain paths were barely accessible and few people ever ventured into the area. It was the ideal location for the *yamabushi* to regroup and eventually settle. For a time many other political refugees, dissidents, persecuted Taoist and Buddhist priests on the run, wandered into the isolated area

seeking refuge in the *yamabushi* encampments. Gradually, over a period of about 400 years, the huge encampments split into clans. Whole families began to emerge through intermarriage, and the few hundred original *yamabushi* became numbered in their thousands.

In total isolation, generation after generation of *yamabushi* lived, worked and died. Every skill that they possessed was put to good and effective use. The military treatise *The Art of War* was studied, assimilated and then applied, its advice being effective when snooping imperial soldiers entered the mountains in search of escaped political prisoners. Many of these imperial search parties, once they had strayed into the Iga region, were never seen again.

The *yamabushi* raised families and studied the teachings and philosophies of Buddhism. Within the framework of Shugendo Buddhism is a sect called Shingon (true word). Shingon is heavily influenced by Tantric beliefs and dwells much on mysticism. Central to Shingon belief is 'Dainichi', a Buddha whose name means Buddha of infinite light. To the followers of Shingon, Dainichi is the source of all existence, absolute and permanent. Certain occult rites are practised in Shingon, termed 'Mikkyo', meaning secret knowledge. The Mikkyo constituted teachings involving worship of the spirits of nature (which well suited the *yamabushi* in their mountain wilderness) and also magic, meditation, and most importantly unlocking the secrets of the human mind. These religious practices were aimed at uniting human mental powers with supernatural forces for the purpose of interpreting the secrets of the universe.

Mystical training

Influenced by Tibetan Tantric principles and Indian yoga systems the *yamabushi* devised a method for concentrating all the will and energy into one endeavour at any given moment. This was initiated by employing hand signs involving intricate finger-knitting patterns termed *kuji-in* or energy channelling. *Kuji-in* was the base for what are known as the five manifestations, which are earth, fire, wind, water, and void. These five hand positions were the primers for a further number resulting in 81 positions in all.

The 81 finger-entwining hand positions are able to cover every eventual circumstance in which the ninja may find himself. By calming his mind and adopting a *kuji-in* hand manoeuvre the ninja in a semi-trance-like state could induce all manner of physiological changes within his own body. These included being able to slow down his heartbeat and blood pressure, apply maximum concentration upon any given problem, stay awake with full faculties for amazing lengths of time, and hold his breath for at least three minutes or more. The *kuji-in* helped the ninja adopt the best frame of mind for whatever venture in which he was involved.

Previous page: *Blending in completely with the landscape was the ninja agent's speciality. From a vantage-point in the long grass the ninja could observe (without being seen) any dangers.*

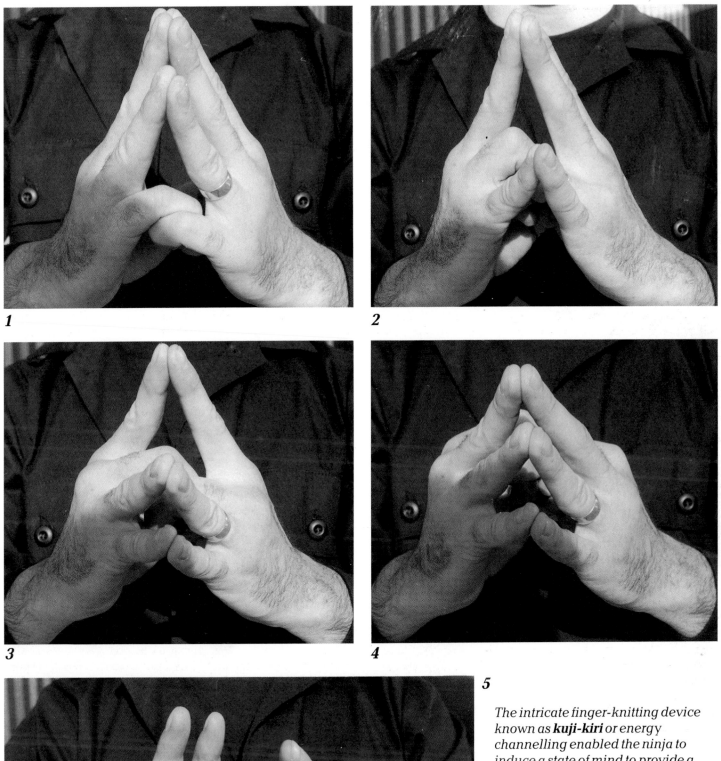

1

2

3

4

5

The intricate finger-knitting device known as **kuji-kiri** or energy channelling enabled the ninja to induce a state of mind to provide a foundation for a particular technique. These finger signs were also called attitudes. The five seen here are **1** earth, **2** water, **3** fire, **4** wind, and **5** void. By forming and concentrating on these hand signals the ninja was able to adopt the right frame of mind for the task at hand. For instance fire is aggressive and fast moving, and is often associated with ninja weapon techniques.

The mystical training in Mikkyo also aided the ninja to increase their own god-given usual five senses, long meditative practices developing their inherent powers of psychic perception. All of these capabilities, and more, created havoc amongst the superstitious feudal peasants, as we shall see. So important is the mental awareness aspect of the Mikkyo teachings that even today ninjutsu training involves the development of such powers.

The golden age of ninjutsu

The centuries rolled by and little was heard from the rebellious mountain priests, ordinary folk thinking that they had long since perished in desolation. At the end of the Heian period, in 1185, the Japanese central government had become so weak that many factions amongst the aristocracy were at work wheeling and dealing. Constant conflicts between lords and religious leaders, all vying for power, provided the perfect setting for the use of spies and assassins to eliminate political adversaries. Thus dawned a time of political unrest called the Kamakura Period (1192-1333), which also became known as 'the golden age of ninjutsu'. With all this power-mongering taking place, utilising the ninja and their special talents, which were well known to a few *daimyo* (lords), seemed like the ideal solution for the feuding officials to call upon in an effort to rid them of opponents. It was during the Kamakura Period that the military dictatorship known as the Shogunate was born, the emperor merely being a figurehead for the country. Along with the Shogunate came the rise to power of the samurai warrior, and their own religion called Zen Buddhism, which laid the foundation for the whole of the samurai culture. Yet culturally the samurai and the ninja were at opposite ends of the scale.

Because of the many private armies that were being organized by the provincial barons, information about troop movements and military strengths and weaknesses was in great demand. The rich lords ruled their areas, making up laws as they went along, leaving their faithful samurai to ensure they were carried out. Consequently, the use of ninja spies became more and more commonplace. For their part, the ninja espionage tactics resulted in the right information reaching the right ears. The lords soon found that one or two agents in the enemy encampment was cheap and that they learned more than a whole army of samurai could glean. Under the cover of darkness or disguised as a wandering priest the ninja moved freely about the enemy's stronghold gathering information about everything. Within a short space of time the ninja became essential for intelligence work — and they soon progressed from information gathering to assassination.

Left: *A Hokusai woodblock print depicting the early use of taijutsu. At the far right a ninja can be seen scaling up a wall on a rope.*

Right: *A Buddhist priest in deep prayer.*

Right below: *A Buddhist and his priests sit in council typical of the meetings held by the Shingon Buddhists of ancient Japanese history.*

Birth of the shadow warrior

Various military generals figured that if a ninja agent could penetrate deep behind the enemy lines, gain access to a camp or castle and then silently slay the army commander or *daimyo* himself, then that particular foe would be leaderless and consequently vanquished, without their armies ever having to meet on the battlefield. This implied a great saving both economically and in terms of human lives. Thus the ninja night assassin, the shadow warrior, was born.

During this 'golden age', the ninja clans blossomed into as many as 70 distinct schools *(ryu)*, with the main strongholds centred in the areas of Iga and Koga provinces. In those days the ninja were known as *shinobi* or stealers-in. Each of the ninja family clans was characterized by its own particular brand of espionage and use of certain weaponry. These specialities were closely-guarded secrets, and each member of a family handed these down through the generations only to members of their own family. For example, a technique known as koppojutsu, which specialized in bone-breaking, was a particular favourite of the Koto clan. The Fudo family were expert in, and responsible for, the development of the star-shaped throwing implement called *shuriken*. Espionage on an elaborate scale was the hallmark of the Kusonoki clan, and later, the great clan of Togakure were adept with the *shuko* and *tetsubishi* (climbing claws and caltrops). In Iga province the two biggest families were Hattori and Oe, who ruled the ninja jointly, whilst to the north in Koga province the clans of Mochizuki, Ukai and Nakai ruled.

By the fourteenth century the ninjutsu organizations had grown in huge numbers, and became great influential and political adversaries of the government. They were no longer content to remain in obscurity in the wilderness and mountains, so they emerged *en masse* and assassinated the *daimyo* that were against them, easily defeating their various armies. The very name of the ninja began to strike fear in the hearts of the aristocracy of the time. The Ashikaga family had seized control of Japan and a period of total disorganization followed. Warfare was rife between rival factions, almost to the point of rebellion and civil war. Groups of nobles and powerful samurai families fought one another for positions of power. Inevitably, by 1500 all of Japan was engulfed by civil war, the country having lost most of its central government due to weak and easily influenced shoguns. In effect the *daimyo* had taken over, each one possessing a self-governing territory in which the ruling lord made all the laws. The next hundred years saw the ninja clans infiltrating in all areas of finance and government. To many, the ninja seemed to be getting completely out of hand. It was said that they had even set their sights on the capital itself.

The ninja's dreaded enemy

At this point a great military general, who had ideas himself of becoming the shogun, appeared on the scene. This was Oda Nobunaga, the dreaded hater and avowed enemy of all ninja. Nobunaga's rise to power seemed to have come almost unnoticed. He had been a petty lord, a minor *daimyo*, then general of a whole army. Aided by his allies he proclaimed himself shogun, and moved into the capital Kyoto. Nobunaga was a fierce and heartless ruler with an excessively cruel streak that resulted in him going on the rampage and declaring war on the Buddhists. He had earlier aligned himself with the new Christian movement that had arrived in Japan some years before via the Jesuits. Although not the slightest bit religious himself, Nobunaga thought that by wiping out the many warlike Buddhist sects he could gain total control of the country. Also, one of the biggest threats at that time was the Shingon Buddhists, who were of course the ninja. In 1571, Nobunaga was responsible for the massacre on Mount Hiei, where with 30,000 troops he put to the sword over 100,000 men, women and children, and razed completely to the ground this ancient religious dwelling place and centre.

For over five years Nobunaga was the scourge of Japan. He massacred and burnt down anything connected with Buddhism. His huge army had gained almost total control of Japan, and slowly the many *daimyo* offered him their allegiance, mainly out of fear rather than liking. Nobunaga's army was the most well equipped and advanced in the country, mainly due to the amount of European muskets it possessed, brought in by the Dutch and Portuguese traders that had arrived with the Jesuits.

Fear in the soul

But still, Nobunaga's greatest fear was that of the ninja clans. Legend relates that his fear arose through an incident in his early life. Nobunaga was out on a hunting trip with a few of his retainers. His travels had taken him into the remote Iga region, heartland of the ninja. Suddenly his horse threw him to the ground. For a few silent moments in the eerie stillness of the fog-enshrouded forest, he is said to have felt a fear that rooted itself in his very soul. For that one instant the myths and tales of the dreaded faceless warriors of the night, the ninja, seemed all too apparent. Although no one was around, he felt totally unprotected and at their mercy. Swiftly climbing back into the saddle he sped away, taking with him this haunting fear.

Many years later, yet still obviously psychologically disturbed by this experience, Nobunaga called to his side his son Katsuyori to lead the army into Iga province and wipe out the ninja clans. In 1579 a vast army of samurai under the leadership of Katsuyori set out to attack the ninja clans. As for the ninja themselves, although outnumbered their clever tactical strategy and guerrilla hit-and-run manoeuvres caused many problems for Katsuyori's army. They finally met head-on in the great battle of Tensho Iga no Ran. The ninja forces proved to be far too clever for the samurai. Using all their ingenuity and warfare skills the ninja soundly beat the invading force and Katsuyori's army retreated with huge losses.

Amidst the dense forest undergrowth, and with drawn swords, two ninja battle for supremacy. Their dull blades clashing, both know that only one of them will live to walk away from this confrontation.

Slaughter of the ninja

This defeat only added fuel to Nobunaga's nervous apprehension of the ninja and two years later in 1581 he made a determined effort in a 'once and for all' bid to wipe out the dreaded black assassins. He personally led a massive force of over 46,000 men to saturate the Iga hinterland with samurai, including crack regiments of musket men – all expert marksmen. Nobunaga's armies outnumbered the ninja clans by more than ten to one and this time Nobunaga was victorious, his sheer overwhelming forces putting the ninja clans on the run. Nobunaga's orders were that everyone should be slaughtered. The ninja losses of men, women and children were staggering. Almost all of the Iga clan was wiped out. The few that managed to escape fled even deeper into the mountains. Here they regrouped and began the slow process of training new warriors in the skills of the ninja. Even so, the once-powerful ninja clans had had their heyday.

A year later the hated Oda Nobunaga was murdered whilst travelling through Honniji territory. Some say that an isolated group of ninja carried out the deed in retaliation for the slaughter of their families. After the death of Nobunaga two generals vied for the leadership. It was eventually decided that Nobunaga's first favourite, a general named Hideyoshi Toyotomi, would rule. One of Hideyoshi's first acts was to prohibit peasants from owning or carrying weapons. He even went as far as to stop the population from changing their occupations, which eventually led to the end of social mobility. Unlike Nobunaga, Hideyoshi despised the Christians and their converts. In 1597 he began a persecution campaign against them, and like his predecessor had behaved towards the Buddhists, Hideyoshi massacred the Christians in their thousands. Hideyoshi saw foreign interference and influence (mostly from the West) as counterproductive to his aim of a united Japan.

Returning a vital favour

Meanwhile the second favourite of Nobunaga, a general named Tokugawa Ieyasu, had been posted to a castle in the east of the country. For him to get to his newly-appointed position he had to travel through the treacherous mountain passes in Iga. The thoughts of journeying through ninja territory after the events of the previous years didn't appeal too much to Ieyasu. So in a clever strategical move, he approached a leading ninja clan chief named Hanzo Hattori for guidance and protection in return for future favours. Hattori saw in this situation a chance to gain power, so he agreed. The ninja chieftain sent out word to the Iga and Koga ninja that Ieyasu's caravan was not to be harmed or stopped, as Hattori himself would be leading it. All the ninja complied with the request and Ieyasu was afforded safe passage. This one act by the ninja leader was to prove very beneficial at a later date.

Exactly one year after the massacre of the Christians, Hideyoshi realized that he had created an almost military caste in the country, giving birth to the rise and power of the samurai. He suddenly found that the feudal lords and *daimyo* were starting revolts. The edict that was issued about carrying arms had caused uprisings and made the collection of local taxes very difficult. All this had begun to interfere with Hideyoshi's expansion plans, and in 1598 the great general died.

Opposite page: *Three ninja stealthily creep up on a deserted beach, but always constantly alert that danger could threaten around any corner.*

Left: *An agent presses himself against an old stone wall and blends in so well with the background that he becomes almost invisible.*

This event had a monumental effect upon the ninja clans. Hideyoshi's successor was Tokugawa Ieyasu, who quickly established himself in control. He set about quelling all the revolts and subduing the *daimyo*. To do this he needed a vast network of espionage agents to inform him of what was going on around the country. This is when the favour by ninja clan chief Hanzo Hattori was returned. The Iga ninja began a huge large-scale operation, infiltrating castles, forts, and all military establishments outside the new capital of Edo (Tokyo), reporting back news and events to Ieyasu about dissident nobles. Thus Hanzo Hattori found himself elevated into the higher echelons of power inside the government.

Peace – and loss of ninja power

Ieyasu, using the ninja agents effectively, reduced insurrection to nil. During this period the shadow warriors were kept very busy spying and carrying out direct assassinations against the feudal lords that would not comply with Ieyasu's dictates. Thus the ninja once again plied their deadly trade with swift justice to all who stood in the way of Ieyasu and the shogunate. In 1603 Ieyasu assumed the title of shogun at Edo. There now followed a series of edicts that had dramatic effects upon Japan, and ironically led to the eventual demise of the ninja as a powerful force.

This period in history became known as the Tokugawa Shogunate. Ieyasu blocked the earlier trade expansion with the West by closing off the country to foreigners. All the ports were shut, except for a small trading post at Nagasaki, run by the Dutch. He ordered that the central government divide the country into 250 feudal areas, each ruled by an overlord. These lords were required to spend a month each year in the capital at Edo. This was done to reduce the possibility of conspiracy. As long as the lords remained loyal to the shogun they were free to operate as they pleased. For the next 260 years Japan became isolated from the rest of the world, and for the first time in centuries civil order was restored and the country was united and at peace.

Unfortunately for the ninja, this peace sealed their end as a dominating power. Hanzo Hattori and his family remained in the employ of the shogun, protecting the shogunate. Hattori organized his ninja into a secret police force and spy system so that Tokugawa Ieyasu could be aware of dissidents and political agitators long before they could ever amount to becoming a threat. The odd ninja or two dispatched at the right time could get rid of any would-be usurpers. But for the mainstay of the ninja clans the peaceful times meant that their work dried up. So the deadly ninja that had been feared for almost ten centuries throughout Japan became little more than gardeners and security guards, their own skills declining along with their art. Many melted into the community doing jobs that their skills best equipped them for. Others found work as farm labourers and put aside the skills of war. For the few ninja that couldn't exist in civilian life they wandered high into the mountains in pursuit of religious activities. Consequently the ninja organizations broke up and disbanded – or so many people thought. A few small groups went underground and continued to practise their skills, handing down to each generation the ways and methods of ninjutsu.

Ninja versus the West

The next time Japan heard of the ninja was in 1853 when the United States sent Commodore Perry and his 'Black Ships' to Japan to open up the country as a trading route. The shogun of the period sent two ninja on board the Western barbarians' ships to steal papers and gain information of what they were really up to. The papers that were stolen proved to be totally insignificant and can be seen today on display in a Tokyo museum.

When Japan adopted the open-door policy for trading, the inevitable flood from the West brought new science and technology to the Japanese. A proper training programme for an army and navy was instigated, samurai were forbidden to wear swords, and feudal Japan entered the twentieth century. In little more than 40 years Japan had caught up with the rest of the world. In the early 1900s Japan had an altercation with the mighty bear of Russia, who had taken Port Arthur. It is without doubt that the Japanese secret service had full knowledge of the exploits of the ninja from long ago, and using their espionage and covert activity methods were successful at gaining pre-knowledge of the strengths and weaknesses of their Russian enemy. They attacked the Russian fleet and were successful; thus again the tactics of the ancient ninja helped win the day. Many people thought that Japan's act of a surprise attack on Port Arthur was not quite fair, as Japan did not declare war on Russia until the next day. But the art of the ninja is the art of winning. Perhaps if they had formally declared their intentions to the Russians, the outcome would have been entirely different.

Into the twentieth century

Surprisingly, not much is known or recorded about the ninja after the Russo-Japanese war, until the late 1960s. In the first few decades of the twentieth century Japan set about a world and trade expansion, which involved them invading China and completely overrunning Manchuria. For such widespread military operations it would be more than reasonable to assume that the tried and tested methods of the ancient ninja were put to full use. Bearing in mind the ninja's ingenuity for adapting anything and everything as a weapon, one can only wonder to what use they put the advanced technology of the 1920s and 30s.

It is known that vast espionage networks were established by the Japanese throughout Manchuria, and certain dissenting Chinese warlords mysteriously disappeared when any kind of contention arose. In the true traditions of the ancient ninja, agents were dispatched to Manchuria long before the Japanese invasion. These spies, acting as a kind of fifth column, would settle in Chinese towns and villages, gaining employment in all walks of Chinese life. They constantly reported anything that might be of interest to the Japanese secret service, in an effort to make the impending invasion run more smoothly. Such information included troop strengths in certain areas, location of munitions factories and supply routes, the mood of the people, how best to use propaganda as a weapon – in fact anything at all that could somehow be used for subversion.

Heavily involved with Japanese secret service activities around that time was an organization called the Black Dragon Society, also known as the Amur River Society. It has been suggested that this society's early beginnings stem from a ninja clan that went underground some 200 years previously, although its founding is credited to the early part of this century. Unfortunately, due to the very nature of ninja activity and organization, little has been documented – and even less is known – about such groups as the Black Dragon and its contemporaries.

It seems a strange paradox that although history can recall many of the ninja clans' exploits up until around 1650, any information after that time seems to be nonexistent. But then, a secret once told ceases to be a secret. And a ninja once discovered ceases to be effective. So it would seem only reasonable to assume that, given the advent of modern communications and espionage methods, the ninja's pathological need for secrecy went even deeper. We have only to look at their Western counterparts in the CIA and MI5. If their every covert activity was documented and made public knowledge, these organizations would cease to be effective almost immediately.

So to all intents and purposes history would have us believe that the ninja clans ceased to function as an organization with the coming of the Tokugawa Shogunate. However, to accept this as fact would be naive. A foundation of nearly a thousand years' experience in espionage, covert activities and political assassination – not to mention a huge well-oiled propaganda machine that was constantly being put to use to keep the common people in check by fear tactics – just would not be wasted simply because a time of peace prevailed. Let us go back to Sun Tsu's *Art of War,* which points out that through a well-laid-out and well-placed espionage system a government can be overthrown without the bloodying of swords. Thus there is little doubt that Hanzo Hattori's early work of setting up a nationwide government espionage system with his ninja clans for Tokugawa Ieyasu heralded the beginning of a highly organized Japanese secret service. We can only conjecture as to what extent the ninja were employed in World War II. It has even been suggested by some contemporary martial arts historians that the plans to assassinate General McArthur were ninja inspired.

Ninja lives today

In the 1980s the martial arts world has seen a great revival of the arts of the ninja. Unfortunately, in the 1960s, before the West could establish the credibility of ninjutsu as a martial art, commercialism reared its head, saw the potential of this ancient warrior caste, and began to market in a sensational way its ancient forms of assassination and subversion. The greatly exaggerated exploits of the ninja agent on film and television laid the foundation for the true ninja arts being held up to a certain amount of ridicule within world martial arts circles. Then in the early seventies the efforts of two men, Doron Navon from Israel and Stephen K. Hayes from the United States, who both trained to instructor level in Japan, gave this once black art the official seal of approval in the West.

Left: Doron Novon of Israel with the grandmaster of ninjutsu Dr Masaaki Hatsumi. The master is executing an inside sword slash across his student's abdomen and kidneys.

Below: Stephen K. Hayes of the USA – often hailed as the father of American ninjutsu and perhaps the art's most ardent crusader in the Western world – in a classical ninja sword stance.

Following page: A group of ninja face each other for a session of sword practice. Constant repetition of techniques was needed in order for the ninja agents to retain their sharp abilities with weapons. The ninja training instructor looks on with a discerning eye, ever ready to remonstrate with a student's lack of skill.

Both these Western pioneers of ninjutsu trained under Japanese ninja master Dr Masaaki Hatsumi. Dr Hatsumi is the 34th grandmaster of what has been described as the oldest remaining historically traceable ninja organization in the world, the Togakure Ryu Ninja. Grandmaster Hatsumi inherited his title from the 33rd grandmaster, Toshitsugu Takamatsu, upon the latter's death. It is only by the efforts of Dr Hatsumi that ninjutsu became known to the Western world, since until the death of his own master the art of ninjutsu was kept totally underground as a secret tradition and only taught to students privately.

Another ninja clan, that of the Koga Ryu Ninja, is also said to exist and still be training in the warrior arts. But if this is true then they are still maintaining the tradition of their ancestors by remaining strictly secret and underground. Koga ninja instructors openly teach in the West, but a central point of Japanese instructional reference has never yet been ascertained.

As to how many other ninja organizations are in existence is anyone's guess. Secrecy, after all, is still at the heart of the ninja.

2

The Pursuit of Excellence is a Lifelong Endeavour

TRAINING TO KILL

In historical terms the *shinobi* or ninja warrior inherited his profession at birth. The young ninja started his or her apprenticeship in the arts of stealth and mayhem almost from the cradle. From early childhood, the children of ninja families were conditioned to be constantly aware of everything around them, the laws of nature being their permanent companions. For by being tuned in, as it were, to natural events and phenomena, a greater understanding could be developed of the elements. This knowledge could then be put to good use to effect either an escape or evasion tactic or as a psychological weapon against the superstitious peasants, who deemed even a simple eclipse of the sun as some form of evil portent from the *kami* (gods).

Deadly games

From about the age of four or five, ninja children's games were channelled around serious training exercises. A child's abilities were carefully observed and then tested to see if they had any inborn skills or special traits. Those with talent were nurtured to hone their inherent skills to almost epic proportions. A modern-day similarity can be witnessed with the Soviet athletes who are taken at an early age and rigorously trained for years to achieve peak Olympic performances. All the ninja childhood games stressed subtle training points that, although not immediately evident, would prove to be most important at a later date in their lives. Games that encouraged balance and agility were at the top of the list. Running up inclined planks and leaping over low bushes, or hanging from the branches of trees by their arms for hours on end, taught

them the feeling of pain and at the same time how to maintain a strong sense of self-discipline by not letting go.

In the ninja encampments, which resembled small villages, experts were on hand in every conceivable skill to teach and train the ninja children. These instructors would have more than likely been field ninja that at one time or another had either injured themselves or been maimed during a mission and yet survived. Every morning and evening the children's young muscles, although still only gristle, would be worked upon by experts in massage to keep their bones and joints flexible. This was done so that in later life, out in the field on a mission, should they be captured and tied up, a simple disjointing of the limb would effect an immediate release and escape to freedom. Massage in Eastern countries, especially in Japan, has usually been the domain of women. So it is more than likely that the female ninja, known as *kunoichi*, were the ones that carried out this task.

Freedom to train and fight

Each year in the life of a child ninja some other skill was added to their already greatly expanding repertoire of techniques. It is difficult for us in the West to conceive the continuous training programme of a ninja throughout the centuries. Morning, noon – and well into the night – the ninja children trained and trained in an effort to reach as near ultimate perfection as possible. To try to understand the thinking behind this intensive training regime we must remember the times that the ninja lived in. Feudal Japan was oppressed and the state dictated everything. Unless of noble birth, the average Japanese could only expect a life of toil and austere existence. Life was cheap, and the slightest affront to anyone higher than the station you were born to, could mean instant death. Examined in these terms, perhaps the life of a ninja wasn't quite as bad as that of his counterpart, the feudal farmer working in the fields from dawn to dusk. At least the ninja had the freedom of the forests and mountains, with all the security of belonging to a family unit.

A classical training exercise for ninja children, aimed at developing their stamina and which produced the ability to run swiftly, was that of speed travelling. This involved the use of a peasant's straw hat, which was placed on the child's chest as the young ninja set off running. If he could keep the hat pressed firmly up against his chest by the force of the wind only, through running very fast, then that was satisfactory enough for his teachers to advance the young ninja to a higher level of training.

The ninja agent had to be a superior runner, not only to elude pursuers but also to carry important intelligence reports which they had gathered, back to their superiors. It must be pointed out that in feudal Japan horses were not freely available: it was usually only the nobles and high-ranking military who were seen on horseback. A mounted horseman other than the two types mentioned, would more than likely bring too much attention to himself – and that's the last thing any ninja agent would want to do. Good strong legs and unlimited stamina would give the ninja field agent an effective retreat avenue. It is said that a ninja could run more than 50 miles non stop in one day. This may seem an awesome feat, but bear in mind that it is only twice the distance of a modern-day marathon, and many people find no difficulty with that. Add to this the fact that the ninja trained for around 18 years to accomplish his many amazing feats of stamina, and his accomplishment at 50 miles a day doesn't seem too daunting or unbelievable.

Superhuman shadow warriors

Constant body conditioning and training brought the ninja warrior up to a maximum peak of fitness and physical endurance, and it is easy to understand why the simple country folk thought that these shadow warriors were almost superhuman. Continous daily training without let up, sustained and carefully monitored diet, expert training in armed and unarmed combat skills, residing in the safety of a family unit during their formative years, and living continually to be at one with the elements next to nature, were ideal ingredients for producing a race of superhumans. The ninja's finely-honed skills and powers enabled them to squeeze through near-impossible openings, hold their breath for very long periods underwater, swim vast distances at high speed, and dive from great heights off cliff tops.

Mountain lakes were where young ninja students learned all the tricks necessary to gain entrance to a castle to carry out their missions. They were trained to move through the water silently with scarcely a ripple to be seen. The young ninja also practised fighting, with and without weapons, in the water. Water-evasion techniques became

just another speciality in the arsenal of acquired skills for the ninja. A ninja knew exactly at what depth he must swim underwater to avoid the arrows of his pursuers, and in later years the musket balls of the rifleman.

Breathing and breath control, which the ninja had learned from childhood, were probably based on Indian yoga systems. It seems likely that the methods came to Japan via China, brought there by the Taoist mystics who spent all their lives experimenting with elaborate breathing techniques in their quest for immortality. To a ninja, the ability to suppress his breathing capabilities was useful in many ways. For example, when a ninja went into hiding, especially near a position occupied by the enemy, the slightest sound, if detected, may well have proven to be his last. If the soldiers' dogs were near, even inhaling and exhaling could prove fatal. Many stories abound in Japanese folklore of how the ninja escaped by using their method of shallow breathing to feign death. Some ninja even reduced their breathing by entering into a yoga-type hypnotic trance.

Previous page: *Climbing ability and superb balance were required by ninja field agents so they could surmount any difficulty or obstacle that lay in their path.*

Right: *Remote and out-of-the-way areas were used as training grounds for the ninja students to practise their deadly skills. Far from prying eyes the ninja warrior learned and perfected his superhuman skills.*

Below: *A ninja field agent's whole aim was to get in, spy or kill, and then get out again without ever being detected.*

A ninja warrior, after locating his target for assassination, hides in the dense undergrowth awaiting the opportune moment to pounce. Striking from nowhere and disappearing in the same manner not only confused the enemy but also gave rise to the legend that the ninja could make himself invisible.

Alertness equalled survival

Throughout all ninja training the one constant that remained uppermost was the necessity to gain the 'edge'. For by always having a great knowledge of the enemy and his capabilities the ninja could fall back on his training and handle each situation with a set course of procedure and action. The field ninja lived on his wits, and was constantly alert within his environment. Consequently, everyday happenings that most people just took for granted could mean an awful lot to the astute ninja agent.

By being trained to recognize a myriad of different sounds without actually ever seeing the person or object making that sound, the ninja could detect impending danger. By being able to assess any noise he heard, such as a door being opened or closed, or footsteps heard in the distance, he could judge not only in which direction they were coming from but also what type of person he had to deal with. The swish of leather against bamboo, heard however softly, could perhaps indicate that a samurai was approaching and this sound of the leather thongs on his armour pressing against the samurai's breastplate would

have prepared the ninja for a surprise assault.

As the ninja child reached his formative years he would be able to enter a room full of sleeping people and instantly judge, by listening to them breathe, how many bodies were in the room. To the trained ear the tell-tale rhythmic breathing of the sleeping people also enabled the ninja to distinguish a light or heavy sleeper, and a false sleeper from a genuine one. It is by being aware of even the most minute details that the ninja was able to slip quietly and unseen into the most fortified castles and strongholds and successfully accomplish his mission without detection.

Amongst the many skills in ninja training, none was more important that that of acting. For, like all spies, his very safety depended upon how well he could carry off the particular disguise format that he was adopting in his espionage quest, be it either as a priest, or merchant, or even a *ronin* (masterless samurai). In feudal Japan, movement was very restricted, and samurai border and boundary guards were stationed everywhere. It was an age of suspicion and insurrection and local lords lived in constant fear of invading armies from other areas trying to

overthrow them and take their lands as their own. If a traveller did not have a bonafide reason for being in an area he was either killed or taken prisoner. It was in this kind of atmosphere that the ninja agent had to try to ply his trade. So merely by dressing up and looking like a priest or merchant just wasn't enough. They had to be completely proficient in the mannerisms and accomplishments of the people whose guise they had adopted. A wandering Buddhist or Shinto priest was usually welcome at all courts and castles. So a ninja in this guise would have to be expert in religious ceremonies and rites in order to carry off his disguise with success.

To many people the time involved in learning the skills of ninjutsu seems extraordinarily long, but when you consider that the hundred and one things they had to master would in future save their lives on many occasions, then the time becomes irrelevant. Constant updating of techniques was implemented when new ideas and recent technical innovations were discovered. This updating included changes in both weaponry and warfare and also in civil advancements.

A captured ninja agent is put to torture by samurai warriors trying to force information from him. Usually there was little point in this as ninjas were sworn to secrecy and no amount of torture would ever lead them to divulge the secrets of their camps.

The 18 areas of expertise

A the height of the historical ninja period, the Togakure ninja clans were trained in 18 areas of expertise which progressed from basic weapon skills to more advanced realms of mental and psychic abilities. But always in ninja training the purity of the soul was most important, sometimes referred to as the 'ninja heart'. The 18 levels were:

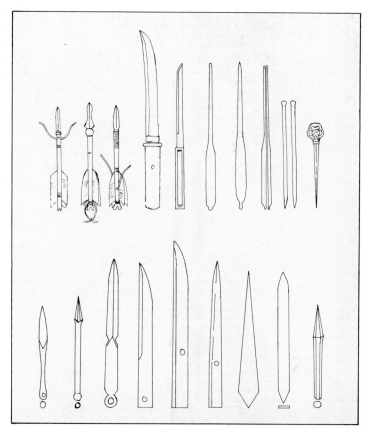

1. Spiritual refinement, which involved the ninja coming to terms with his strengths and weaknesses, and intention, commitment and personal motivation. Being part philosopher through the mystical teachings of the Shugendo, the ninja strived to put himself in touch with the universal laws of nature.
2. Unarmed combat, involving grappling and escaping, plus rolling and leaping.
3. Ninja sword, involving fast-draw sword techniques and cutting and attacking.
4. Stick and staff fighting, involving use of 6 ft and 4 ft (1.8 m and 1.2 m) staffs and the *hanbo*.
5. *Shuriken* throwing.
6. Spear fighting.
7. *Naginata* techniques, involving fighting with the halberd.
8. Chain and sickle weapons.
9. Fire and explosives, including demolition and distraction methods.
10. Disguise and impersonation, including personality traits and career roles.
11. Stealth and entering methods, combining silent movements with breaking and entering.
12. Horsemanship.
13. Water training, involving swimming and floating.
14. Strategy, including unconventional tactics, deception, political plots and influencing events.
15. Espionage, including recruiting spies and setting up espionage cells.
16. Escape and concealment, involving camouflage and invisibility techniques.
17. Meteorology, involving forecasting and taking advantage of the weather conditions.
18. Geography, including terrain features, map-making and combat strategy.

Ninja children were brought up to become the perfect – or as near perfect as possible – killing machine. Only the mission mattered, all else was unimportant. Their total devotion to this aim knew no bounds. This was instilled into them almost from the time they could comprehend the spoken word. Each skill learned brought them a step nearer to becoming a total warrior, able to survive the hardships of harsh weather, fight off the enemy who were sometimes three and four strong, withstand great pain under torture (if they were captured), and yet never divulge anything they knew – even to the point of committing suicide rather than betray the clan.

Below: *Stephen Hayes adopts a striking pose with the most ancient of all weapons, the **bo** staff. The ninja's technical ability with a staff had to be so highly refined that if he were to be attacked by sword-wielding samurai he could still be successful at defeating them.*

Above: *American ninja master Stephen K. Hayes employing the ninja's self defence art of taijutsu (body art), locking a young student in a grip. Hayes, by dropping his own knee in a stooping manner behind that of the student's, forces the student to fall backwards.*

Above left: *A varied assortment of throwing shafts used by the many different **ryu** (schools) of ninjutsu. Each school had a specific design to their throwing darts or **shuriken**.*

Below left: *A ninja agent with a varied assortment of weapons employed on missions, including the **shuriken** or pointed throwing darts, spears, his **katana** or sword, climbing claws, and the iron truncheon-like weapon known as the **sai**, which were used in pairs.*

The art of stealth

The very name ninjutsu means stealing-in or stealth art. So a ninja had to be expert in creeping around stealthily. For without a sound an assassin could become almost invisible, able to move about the old wooden castles of Japan with their creaking floorboards, yet never be discovered. In order to perfect those talents, ninja training devised certain techniques of walking. For instance in a movement known as *yoko aruki,* they learnt to walk by moving their legs sideways in a cross-step fashion. Tracks left in this manner do not readily reveal in which direction a ninja is travelling and thus confuse a pursuing enemy.

Ninja children, almost from the time they left the cradle to take their first steps, were taught to tread carefully and lightly. This training would often begin by them having to walk repeatedly through a shallow pool of water without making a splash and barely a ripple. Another method used when the children became older and more advanced, was to lay wet rice paper on the floor, which the ninja students were required to walk up and down on without the soles of their feet ripping or tearing the paper.

As training continued in its never-ending series of learning, the ninja was taught how to read simple maps and gain the skill of actual map-making. This skill was necessary because, apart from the assassinations the ninja carried out, espionage, spying and gleaning information of troop movements were very much part and parcel of his everyday field of activities. For this intelligence work to be carried out effectively, the ninja had to be able accurately to sketch maps indicating the terrain, the deployment of troops and the enemy's position in general in relation to the area in which they were camped. Sometimes a ninja would be employed to create a diversion and slow down an advancing enemy, which was relatively easy for him to accomplish. A simple trick of poisoning the water that the horses drank would create catastrophic consequences, and hold up an advancing army long enough for the hunters to become hunted themselves. This kind of fifth-column activity was the hallmark of the ninja field warrior.

Insert: *Becoming at one with nature, the ninja could adopt a camouflage position in the undergrowth and by keeping absolutely still with carefully controlled breathing techniques he could remain undetected for as long as he wished.*

Quite often, if the mission dictated, ninja agents would work in groups of three or more. A group of ninja, emerging from the undergrowth, begin to lay out plans for their infiltration behind enemy lines.

Psychological weapons

As the ninja children's knowledge accumulated, so too did their lessons. With age came comprehension and understanding and the subtleties of human nature were explored in the ninja's advanced psychology classes. Obviously lessons of this nature had to be left until the children were of an age to appreciate the using of another man's greed or jealousy to pry out information and female ninja children, called *kunoichi*, were taught how to use their charms in more amorous ways.

It was important for the ninja to be skilled in the use of dialects, since one of the biggest giveaways would be when a ninja, operating far from his base, suddenly began to converse in a dialect that was alien to the particular part of the country in which he was operating. This danger would be heightened if the ninja's standard line of conversation didn't correspond with his disguise. The absolutely vast number of skills learned in the 18 to 20 years a ninja trained can only be measured by the continuing success they had as assassins and espionage agents for a thousand years.

Power of darkness

Although much has been written about the ninja only fighting at night, much of their work was actually done in the hours of daylight. As information-gatherers they would wander around village markets picking up on any conversation that would have aided them in their ultimate mission. However, gaining entry into a castle was obviously best left to the twilight hours. The military governing powers prohibited all movement by the common people in the hours of darkness, so at least the ninja knew that any sounds or gathering of people could only be soldiers or samurai. Knowing this, and treating every noise as a potential danger to himself, he was well prepared for instant retaliation.

With no light to guide him the ninja needed incredible night vision powers. It is therefore not unreasonable to assume that he ate vast amounts of watercress, which grew plentifully around the rivers and streams, to gain the valuable vitamin A for his eyesight. As a child the ninja would have to spend hours at a time in very small totally dark confines, in order to get his eyes used to the dark. Thus in later years, when out on assignment, he could operate at ease in the blackness of the night.

A ninja field agent would never fight just for fighting's sake. His whole aim was to get in, complete his mission, and then get out again without ever being seen. But even with the best laid plans, the unexpected can happen. So the ninja, when confronted, had to fight his way out by whatever means possible. The skills he used in self-defence, both armed and unarmed, were truly awesome. Anything that came to hand became a weapon for the ninja to use in the protection of his life. A ninja's life was fraught with danger from dawn to dusk, from birth to grave. The more knowledgeable he became, the better his chances of surviving for the next assignment . . .

Far left: *A female ninja, called* **kunoichi,** *in the taijutsu stance known as the receiving position. From this position she can employ a simple body manoeuvre to repel an unarmed attack from an adversary.*

Left: *As well as rope, steel claws were used for climbing. Even the thick ninja swordguard provided a footing when the scabbard was placed against a wall.*

THE INVISIBLE WARRIOR

When they think you are near, be far. When they think you are far, be near

(Sun Tsu)

Living a rugged life as a virtual outcast from society, the ninja learned to acclimatize his body to the weather of all the seasons and dressed accordingly. For instance, in the winter months he would don his garb of white so as to become virtually invisible in the snow. His brown-hued ninja suit in the autumn months would blend well with the falling leaves of the forest. Being able to blend in with his surroundings at any given moment fed the ninja legend over the years of his ability to disappear at will.

The best hours of operation for the ninja who wished to remain unseen were naturally those of darkness, which permitted him to merge in with natural or other backgrounds. For very important and critical assignments, the ninja prepared his vision by keeping himself in the dark for at least 24 hours prior to his mission. His daylight hours would be spent deep in a dark cave, thus creating a fine night-sight sensitivity. It was this kind of cunning, deception and total dedication to his mission that was often to give the ninja the edge over his enemies. For the ninja, however, being invisible did not necessarily entail not being seen, in the strict sense of the word. Invisibility can also mean going undetected as to one's true intentions and the ninja in disguise, acting as a travelling priest or merchant, was 'invisible' to his enemy.

Planning a mission

The whole of the ninja clan structure centred around the success of the ninja field agent himself. These family systems were organized along strict military lines, with a hierarchy, rather than a father, governing everything. The ninja were divided into three ranks: the *jonin*, who were the leaders; the *chunin*, who were the subleaders or lieutenants; and finally at the bottom of the scale the *genin* who were the operational field agents, also known as ninja or *shinobi*.

The *jonin* maintained an extensive intelligence network. They made contact with the warlords and *daimyo* who wanted subversive or espionage missions carrying out. Once the brief for the mission had been established, it would be given to a contact who had connections with a ninja clan. The contact then met the *jonin* concerned and the job was accepted.

All the necessary details would be ironed out between the *jonin* and the *chunin* (middleman). It was up to the *chunin* to select a *jonin* or field ninja to go out and perform the task. As for the ninja agent himself, the fee for his services, or degree of impossibility of the task, were none of his concern. If selected, his only intention would be the 'mission' and its successful completion. Failure did not even enter into the *genin*'s mind – he was either successful or killed; these were the only two options that existed. Bearing in mind this almost psychotic attitude to duty, we can see how the ninja agent in execution of his mission must have been a frightening enemy.

For the ninja, being selected for his first mission would be the time when all his childhood training and the vast array of skills learned over the long years came into play. Because the ninja always planned ahead, knowing that for each situation he prepared for there would always be a dozen others he could never foresee, he would make sure he

Left: *Emerging from the icy depths of a castle moat, the ninja will silently scale the high wall and soon be in the private chamber of his unsuspecting victim – ready to administer death.*

Right: *By wrapping himself around the trunk of a tree, the ninja became part of it and thus invisible to his enemies.* Far right: *The ninja warrior carried an awesome array of weapons and gadgets to help him achieve his mission and survive to tell the tale.*

studied the geography of the mission area and its people. Once on his way, the ninja would have selected the special weapons and tools he would need to complete the task. He would have prepared himself for the elements, depending upon the season. If, for instance, it was wintertime, his reversible suit would be worn on the white side, and he would wear heavy metal-bladed sandals to allow him to walk across frozen lakes and rivers. He would build a form of ice igloo to rest in and also plan his manoeuvres to fulfil his mission – and most importantly ensure that he had organized a suitable escape route. Often the ninja's ice house would be erected inside the branches of a low-hanging tree and in the direction of the prevailing wind. This facilitated a build-up of drifting snow which gave him extra cover as well as anonymity. In the more pleasant spring and autumn months, the ninja would dig himself a hole and cover it all over with earth, just leaving a small air hole to breath through.

Focusing the mind on survival

The ninja field agent knew that survival was a state of mind. Correct planning meant that he would live to walk away. In the depths of winter, travelling across the wide open spaces with snow and ice all around and freezing winds chilling him to the marrow, many a lesser person would have just given up. But not the ninja. No matter how barren and bleak his predicament, through bringing into focus the powerful force of his mind and concentrating it on a given problem, he could quickly assess the right action to take in order to stay alive.

Making use of prevailing weather conditions was of prime importance to the ninja. Using the natural elements against the enemy gave him a very high advantage. The ability to recognise and predict weather conditions could sometimes make a lone ninja as effective as an army. If, for instance, the wind was blowing from a certain direction, he could gauge whether or not it was likely to change and

from this knowledge would set fire to an enemy encampment, knowing that the winds would blow towards the camp and fuel the fire even further. A huge army would soon be driven into chaos and confusion at the sight of a swiftly advancing mighty bush fire.

No weather conditions, no matter how severe they seemed, were ever deemed impossible for the ninja to work in. In fact, they welcomed any sort of unusual happenings, because the ninja always performed the unexpected. He took advantage of everything that came his way. Using deceptive ruses combined with good psychology, he flattered vain officials to cajole information from them. If the ninja was dressed as a priest, who in those days acted as news-bringers as well as religious leaders, he would have little difficulty in spreading lies of impending doom or pestilence to news-starved village communities. All this subversion was brilliantly executed – and all to the ends of the ninja. He was invisible in the middle of the enemy, yet created an atmosphere of complete desperation all around him.

Because of a lifetime spent in outdoor training the ninja was adept at wisely using environmental camouflage thoroughly to blend in with the terrain. His ingenious use of storms, fog and other natural phenomena, struck fear even into the hearts of the samurai, who, although brave and fearless men against mortals, had no defence against what they thought were demons or ghosts.

Terror in the bravest heart

Once a ninja entered a castle, he knew that he would come up against light in one form or another, perhaps from the many oil-lamps hung around the samurai barracks or from an open door in one of the castle apartments. So when light did appear at the place where he must enter or work in, the ninja took precautions against casting a tell-tale shadow. With a potential enemy everywhere, each step he took had to be thought through. Problems were many, such as working upwind rather than downwind, lest the castle dogs caught his scent, or making sure an inadvertent sound was not magnified and carried to the castle sentries to alert them of his presence.

The ninja's tricks and ruses were so diverse that even many of the nobles and lords thought that they were sorcerers or magicians who had control over nature. Superstitious villagers spoke about the ninja's occult powers in frightened whispers. Consequently, legends were built up to such an extent that the very mention of a ninja operating in their area struck terror into the bravest heart.

The ninja worked on the concept that deception and surprise would lure the enemy into making false estimates and judgements, which would lead to erroneous military action. So, therefore, when an enemy was united, the ninja divided them; when the enemy was unprepared, the ninja attacked. By knowing how to wear an enemy down, how to keep him under constant strain, and by striking unseen and leaving no trace, it is not difficult to see why the ninja clans of Japan were held in such high esteem by the ruling lords of the period.

At the ninja's mercy

The *daimyo* and lords were always aware that assassination attempts would be an almost regular occurrence. The more important or powerful the lord, then the more dangerous he was to an adversary. So in addition to having huge numbers of personal bodyguards who protected them at all times, they also rigged up little booby-traps in their living quarters as a line of second defence. These early alarm systems could detect an intruder within the private chambers of the castle and alert the samurai guards. This meant that the ninja, once within the castle walls, had to run a virtual gauntlet of both sophisticated and crude burglar alarms, such as doors deliberately left unoiled so that if anyone tried to open one silently, they would be heard all around the halls as the door creaked open. Always prepared for the unknown, the ninja got around this by carrying a small phial of vegetable oil with

him to lubricate squeeky hinges. False floorboards were another trick, some boards having been specially prepared so that the slightest pressure emitted a loud noise. To avoid this the ninja employed a special series of walking techniques, which he had learned all those years before when training on wet rice paper.

Once into the chamber the sleeping lord was at the ninja's mercy. Death could come in an instant by a quick flash of a blade. But because the rich nobles went so much in fear for their lives, it was not unusual for them to be checked by their samurai guards every hour of the day and night. If a noble was discovered murdered, a hue and cry would follow and thus cut the ninja's chances down of effecting a swift and safe escape. So for his own security reasons the ninja would probably despatch the sleeping lord using a slow-acting poison, which he always carried with him.

Right: *The samurai, although among the most deadliest fighters in the world, were often no match for the more skilled ninja.*

とろ臺にて　武藝に達し　就中鎗の名人なり

裏門に鎖縄を提係飛鳥の如く龍入て

にくを聞ければ我劣じと

相戦ふ高教八師直

懸庭傳ひ小馳入しが

ふわりと喩ハりしのら

くらめし頃を臨で礒と

と高教八其身を左へ

志水を修煉の割桃ふ

を勝んで突係る寛に

ーて丁に請止踏込で打太刀を

勢ひ出て神山鬼波の撰り勝負

を獄より志水を目係突係る流石の一學

ふ敵ーぐらく替力労で見ゆる所を高教透きに

の咽ひとぐぎと喫引抜鎗と共偶に潰ゞる血ふ

學八討果ふけり二個八死骸に目を係ぞ

Master of poisons

Being a master of all types of poisons, especially the use of herbal concoctions, the ninja knew every plant and shrub in the forest and which ones contained the most deadly poisons. Some potions were used to paralyse, others as halucinogenics. To a superstitious samurai, another samurai with the effects of a halucinogenic in their system would appear to be possessed of evil spirits and demons. The ninja's knowledge of chemistry and botany can be equated with that of a pharmacist. He may not have had access to the sophisticated poisons or drugs of today, but the organic mixtures he used were just as deadly.

One particular favourite the ninja found regular use for was the poison from the *fugu* or blowfish. In Japan even today this fish is considered a special delicacy, and at certain *fugu*-licensed restaurants one can enjoy this dish. But this fish is so deadly poisonous, the active ingredient called tetradoxin being in its every organ, that the Japanese government issue cooks with a special licence to prepare it.

Fugu poison carried around in a special container could be rubbed upon the lips of the sleeping lord. The poison attacks the respiratory system at the centre of the brain, paralysing the muscles related to breathing. The ninja, having fulfilled his mission, then had ample time to leave the castle without the alarm being raised at the death of the lord. When morning came the quick-acting poison, the effects of which had been slowed down by being applied only to the lips, suddenly reacted and the ninja's mission was complete. Yet although he had made good his escape earlier, he did not leave the vicinity until he knew his mission was a success.

A ninja lies in wait concealed amidst the foliage of a tree, in order to attack an enemy agent he knows is operating in the area. Feudal lords always employed their own retinue of ninja agents for protective purposes.

Left: *A ninja warrior crouched ready to hurl his pointed death star known as a* **shuriken.** *These stars were often tipped with deadly poison.*

Right: *A ninja in full agent's field outfit with sword drawn ready to cut down an adversary. Once discovered the ninja warrior would fight tooth and nail in order to survive.*

Making good his escape

The mission completed, he would set off on the long journey back to the clan encampment. He knew that all the border guards would have been alerted and search parties would be out hunting him. The ninja's expertise in surviving outdoors against the elements, and also against all odds, was legendary. Through his early extensive training he could exist alone in the wilds on a day-to-day basis. Sometimes if an escape route was blocked, the ninja would have to travel many miles out of his way in order to be free. The rations he would have originally taken with him for the job would probably have run out and to get home he would have to live off the land.

The woods and fields were the ninja's kitchen. The Japanese *daikon* or giant radish grew in abundance so he could sustain himself off the land. A substance made from soya beans called *tofu* was easily digested and rich in protein and the ninja often carried this about on his person as an emergency ration. As an expert in nutrition the ninja was wary of heavy foods such as greasy or oily meats which take a long time to digest and have the effect of making the body sluggish, giving a feeling of lethargy and consequently slowing him down. A balanced diet was essential if he were to survive out in the wilds. Thus it wasn't just a matter of the ninja eating anything that was available: he had to be particular.

Often in making an escape the ninja agent could fall foul of a skirmish with the enemy and become injured. If he was wounded or ill in any way, with no doctor at hand, he could possibly die. In this situation his knowledge of pharmacy was vital. He knew of certain types of mushrooms growing in the forest, such as the puffball fungi, which would cure him of infected wounds. The puffball emits a dust when squeezed that is rich in an antibiotic not unlike penicillin. A sword cut quickly healed when this forest medicine was applied.

Constantly being pursued the ninja avoided all signs of civilization, keeping only to the desolate and secluded areas for fear of being seen. In an alien environment the ninja kept a constant look-out for the tell-tale signs of habitated areas. As an expert tracker he knew that ruts on the pathways meant that farmers had pulled their carts along and so this was a route to be avoided. Spirals of smoke through the trees told him that a hut or house was nearby. If he was completely lost in an area that was totally new to him, the ninja would look around for a felled tree or even fell a small one himself just so that he could examine the rings on the tree stump. This he knew acted as an excellent direction finder since the rings always grow biggest and peak in the direction of the south.

The ninja warrior was never at a loss at keeping himself alive by one means or another. When a ninja was thirsty and could not get to water for fear of being discovered, he would suck a type of lozenge made from peppermint powder which would slake his thirst until water was found. Yet a ninja's sense of awareness was honed to razor sharpness to such an extent it is said that like an animal he could smell water from a great distance.

Killing the pursuing enemy

Once his pursuers were perhaps gaining on him he would examine what options were open to him. He could maybe try to out-run them, but if they were mounted samurai this could prove a little difficult. Faced with such a predicament the ninja would enter a dense part of the forest and set about arranging a series of booby-traps. In the dark depths of the forest the ninja was on home ground. All his lifetime's experience came to the fore as he thought up devastating traps to ensnare and kill his pursuing enemy. Stakes with sharpened ends tipped with animal dung would be concealed in the dense undergrowth and these had the effect of poisoning the bloodstream. Small gullies would be dug out and covered with leaves so that the pursuers' horses would trip, breaking their legs. Sapling trees would be bent back and secured with vines on a hidden trip wire running across a pathway. Once this wire was disturbed the sapling would fly out and whack the horsemen off their mounts. A myriad of such devices was available to the ingenious ninja warrior, for in the half-light and shadows of the forest, the pursuers were in his domain and often at his mercy.

If no forests were near, and his pursuers were homing in fast, the ninja would simply hide by using his special techniques of self-camouflage. This entailed the ninja blending in with his surroundings at any given moment. He would dash behind a tree stump or a rock and become part of that object. Because of the subtle training methods he had studied as a child he was able to concentrate his mind and focus it towards melting into his surroundings. Once in that state he could shape his body to correspond to his environment. He would curl up into a ball and look just like another stone or boulder, which would prove very confusing to his pursuers looking for a man with arms and legs. By wrapping himself around the trunk of a tree, the ninja assumed the pose of a tree and became part of it. Being able to remain motionless for extended periods of time, his pursuers would simply ride right past him without noticing.

The ninja with three wives

The great lengths that a ninja took to remain free have been the source of many legends. History has recorded that a famous ninja named Sandayu Momochi, who was a founder of the Iga ninja, maintained three different homes, each with a wife and family. In these homes he adopted a different lifestyle. For instance, in one city he would be a merchant, in another he was lamp maker, and the third saw him as a farmer. In creating this situation for himself his anonymity was assured. He could operate in one area and if discovery seemed likely he would disappear and emerge 50 miles away as another person complete with wife and family. This ruse was so successful that in 1581 when the ninja-hater Lord Oda Nobunaga sent out his 46,000 troops against the ninja clans, Sandayu escaped and assumed one of his alternative identities. He kept these tricks up all his life and was never captured.

Sandayu had many students in his lifetime, but his greatest was a man called Goemon Ishikawa, who has been called the bandit hero of Japan and is often likened to Robin Hood. Unfortunately for this unlikely hero neither the Iga nor Koga ninja would acknowledge him as their own, because he used his ninja skills for personal gain rather than for the benefit of the clans.

Perhaps the most famous of all the ninja was Hanzo Hattori who ended his days in the service of the great shogun Ieyasu, and is credited as the founder of the Japanese secret service. In one of the many tales that surround his escapades, Hattori is said to have built a type of paddle-boat with a huge saw on the bow. This boat was used to destroy the early wooden submarines that had been sent against his shogun by rival ninja factions.

Merciless torture

Even after long years of training, the ninja agents were deemed expendable by the hierarchy of *chunin* and *jonin*. So it was therefore in the ninja's own hands whether or not he survived on a mission. Occasionally a ninja agent was caught whilst executing his mission. He knew that if this happened he would be tortured mercilessly and put to death very slowly, his captors doing everything in their power to make him talk before he died. The ninja clans had an iron-clad law or code of discipline that forbade divulging information. He was sworn to secrecy about his training, his contacts, and of course the whereabouts of the main ninja encampment. Thus the ninja preferred death (often by his own hand) rather than betray his fellow warriors. Any ninja who was disloyal was ruthlessly hunted down by other members of the clan and put to death. So strong was this code of honour, that if a small group of ninja was operating in an area and it looked as though one of them might be caught, he would be killed instantly by his own associates before they made good their own escape.

Finally the ninja agent, after completing his mission and evading his pursuers, arrived back at his own encampment. The fees for the assassination or information gathering would be paid to the *jonin*. As for the field agent himself, his only reward was the knowledge of a job well done and to be welcomed back into the fold of the ninja clan family unit, to be fed and clothed, sheltered and warmed — until the next mission.

*The 34th grandmaster of Togakure ninjutsu, Masaaki Hatsumi, in his younger days. He is seen here forming the energy-channelling finger-knitting method of **kuji-kiri**.*

Far left and left: *Adaptability was vital for the ninja's survival – often involving a change of clothing determined by the weather conditions.*

4
DEADLY WEAPONS

**A Single False Move Loses
The Game**

The ninja and their art of ninjutsu employed a vast collection of weird and wonderful weapons. If ever a man could be termed a walking arsenal, it would certainly be the ninja warrior. On his missions he carried an awesome array of weapons and gadgets that would aid him defeating an enemy. Because the ninja's missions often took him hundreds of miles away from his own area, and he would not know what facilities were available to him at his destination, he had to carry everything he needed on his person.

All the ninja's weapons were of a very distinct nature. Many had dual purposes to cut down on travelling weight. They had to be extremely effective yet light, and concealable enough to be carried inside the ninja's uniform, called a *shinobishozuki*. To carry a back pack or rucksack of some description would have meant bringing attention to himself and therefore raise questions. So unless the job was of a particular specialist nature the ninja went off into the night with both hands free.

The ninja sword

Perhaps the most readily identifiable weapon of the ninja was his sword or *shinobikatana*. The ninja sword was totally different to that of the samurai's beloved weapon. It was generally short (about 20 inches – 50 cm – in length), having a single-edged straight blade with an oversized handguard (*tsuba*). Because the blade was short the ninja could strap it to his back and thus keep his hands free. If he were suddenly attacked the sword could be unsheathed whilst still on his back and put quickly into action. The low

ceilings in Japanese houses prohibited a very long sword being drawn in this manner, but a short, straight 20 inch blade proved to be no problem.

Everything about the ninja's sword was a veritable box of tricks. The scabbard was longer than the blade by about 3 inches (7.5 cm). This extra space allowed the ninja to store poisons, powdered medicines and flash powders in its detachable bottom. If he was pursued by enemy soldiers he could remove this lower piece of the scabbard, dive into a river or lake and use the hollow scabbard to breath through. Over and over again, tricks such as these not only confused the enemy but laid the foundation for ninja being thought of as superhuman spirits that could disappear at will.

The long cord used for strapping on the sword could be put to a multitude of uses, for instance as a rope to tie up a prisoner or in conjunction with the extra large handguard for helping the ninja over some high obstacle such as a castle wall. Stepping on to the sword's *tsuba*, this extra leg-up could then be aided by the ninja hurling the rope over a parapet and pulling himself up with it. In the forest he could snare small game using the cord as a slip-knot noose.

The sword had a very different meaning for the ninja than it did for the samurai. The samurai carried two swords which, along with his top-knotted hair, was the mark of a warrior. His trusty *katana* (swords) were made from high-grade carbon steel and each had taken months to make by skilled swordsmiths, who hammered and folded and hammered again the edge of the blade until it contained hundreds of layers of finely-forged steel. The reverence a samurai placed upon such a weapon was little short of worship. His blade was his very being, his honour, his code, even his soul. The ninja's sword, on the other hand, had a blade that was of very poor quality and dull in comparison to the razor-sharp edge of the samurai blade. It resembled nothing more than a short piece of sharpened iron with a handle and was crudely forged using less than ideal materials. The finished product often had a tendency to break. To the ninja, his sword was just another tool of the trade.

A hundred and one weapons

If a ninja was confronted out in the open by a samurai he was at an immediate disadvantage if he had to rely on his sword alone. But the ninja had plenty of other nefarious little weapons concealed about his person to more than even up the odds. When a ninja did use his short sword to fight with, he also employed the scabbard as well, which could be used for blocking and countering.

Throughout his childhood training the ninja would have been taught to master a hundred and one different types of weapons. *Bo* staffs, sticks and canes were all regarded as important weapons. An ordinary *bo* staff (6 foot – 1.8 m – pole) in the hands of a ninja disguised as a wandering Buddhist priest could suddenly be turned into a devastating arsenal of hidden weapons. Before the startled adversary could react, the priest cum ninja, with a quick flick of the wrist, could propel a small sharp missile into the chest of his enemy from the hollowed out *bo* staff which was spring loaded. The versatile *bo* staff could even be converted into a one-shot musket. If a samurai advanced upon a cornered ninja, the *bo* staff end was flicked off and out would come a lethal swirling chain with which the ninja could ensnare his enemy, then move in close and finish him off with his short black dagger called a *tanto*.

Quite often when confronting a ninja, enemy soldiers preferred not to face him man to man but try and finish him off with a bow and arrow, or by hurling a spear at him. The ninja was so very clever and devious that the ordinary Japanese infantryman would have been too frightened for a one-to-one confrontation.

Chains and cords of death

Another favoured fighting instrument of the ninja was the *kusarigama*, which was a long-range blade and chain weapon. A ninja could hurl the chain with its weighted end at an enemy from a safe distance, entangle him and then move in close with the sickle-shaped blade and cut him to pieces. A similar weapon to that of the *kusarigama*, but used much earlier in ninja history, was the *kyoketsu shoge*. This had a hook blade with an 18-foot-long (5.5 m) length of cord attached to it, with an iron ring fastened on to the opposite end. It was used exclusively by the ninja, and here again the long cord could be put to use in a hundred other ways when not being used as a weapon.

Another ninja weapon in the same vein was called a *kusarifundo* or 'ten thousand power chain'. This consisted of a short length of chain about 20 inches (50 cm) long with two heavy metal weights attached to each end. The *kusarifundo* was easily concealed in the ninja's uniform pocket and could be produced in an instant. One end of the chain is held in the hand and the weight at the other end is hurled outwards in a similar manner to that of a child's yo-yo. The heavy metal ball hits the adversary and stuns him, the ninja then quickly moves in and closes the distance to finish the enemy off with a strangulation technique using the chain. Although a short-range weapon the *kusarifundo* was extremely effective in a tight situation.

Previous page: *Dr Hatsumi poses in one of the many sword stances involved in the sword skills of the ninja. This high raised position guards the whole of the body.*

Far left: *A swordmaker constructing the short-bladed ninja weapon that became so effective in the hands of the skilled field agent.*

Below left: *Ninja chain weapons, which include the* **manrikusari, kusarigama** *and* **kusarifundo.** *These weapons, which were easily concealed inside the ninja's tunic, could be produced in an instant.*

Below: *A superb example of the* **ninja-to** *or* **shinobikatana** *– the ninja sword, although this finely produced modern version bears little resemblance to its original counterpart.*

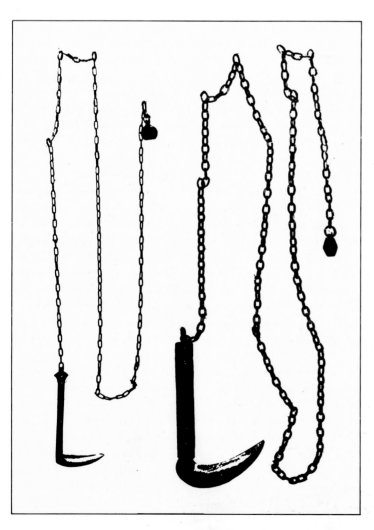

Sowing poisonous seeds

The ninja uniform, called a *shinobishozuki,* consisted of jacket, trousers, hood, and special shoes called *tabi* which were split-toed. Within this garb were many concealed pockets and pouches in which the ninja carried all manner of useful items to aid him on his mission. Each of the ninja clans had their own distinct versions of common weapons. Many were of a specialist nature that wouldn't even be considered a weapon by the ordinary footsoldier or samurai. But to the ninja they could mean the difference between escape and capture.

The *tetsubishi* or caltrop was a small escape and evasion weapon used exclusively by the ninja. This weapon carried a barb similar to those seen on barbed wire and were scattered around a ninja's route of escape, so that when his pursuers gave chase they would tread on the sharp points and fall down in pain. Because the ninja often coated these *tetsubishi* with poison, a pursuing enemy not only fell down in agony but stark fear entered their hearts at the thought of not knowing whether what they had just stepped upon was poisonous or not. Usually this was enough to halt any pursuer from further chasing the ninja.

Using forward planning the ninja could enter a castle and leave *tetsubishi* scattered around a small passageway, which would serve to slow down any pursuer. If the ninja had to jump out of a second-storey window he would, upon landing, let the enemy see him scattering the caltrops. This effectively stopped them following him down, and they would have to give chase from another direction. Should the ninja have cause to scale a wall to make good his escape, once he was over the top he would place a series of caltrops along the wall. A pursuer vaulting up after him would suddenly find his hands impaled on the deadly spikes. Even in hand-to-hand combat, the *tetsubishi* were thrown into the enemy's face to distract him long enough for the ninja to close in for the kill.

It is perhaps interesting to note that the lords and *daimyo* cottoned on to the use of caltrops as a security device and these were often scattered around the hallways at nights to prevent unwelcome visitors from suddenly bursting in. As always the ninja was even prepared for this eventuality. Once he had discovered they were in the vicinity, his special methods of walking allowed him gently to push the caltrops in front of him with the side of his foot. Making no noise he would sweep them along, gaining entrance to the particular room he required and carrying out the deed. In his escape he left the caltrops in their new position, a pursuing enemy then being confronted by his own strewn devices and having no way of knowing if they were the original castle weapons or if the ninja had strewn them – in which case the tips could be poisoned.

Because *tetsubishi* were used in such large amounts it would be impossible for the ninja to carry a large supply on his person. So therefore when he ran out, nature lent a hand. The ninja would go into the forest and gather water chestnut shells, which have a similar shape to the *tetsubishi.* These would then be coated with either animal dung or a poison from his own pocket.

Climbing like a cat

A very prominent ninja weapon that had a dual role was the *shuko.* This implement, which was worn on the hands like a pair of gloves, would allow the ninja to grip very smooth and hard surfaces. It was primarily used for scaling a castle wall to gain entry into his intended victim's chambers. The *shuko,* also known as *tekagi,* was made of one narrow and one wide metal band joined by a flat metal section. The narrow band slipped over the hand and tightened around the wrist, leaving the wide band to encircle the hand. From the palm side upwards of the wider band protruded four sharp spikes.

Apart from these climbing claws giving the ninja access to difficult places and the climbing abilities of a cat, they could be used for close-quarter fighting. If suddenly surprised by a sword-wielding guard on the castle battlements, the ninja could easily block a sword strike to his head by using the *shuko.* In retaliation the ninja could then strike out using the spikes to injure the guard and then make good his escape.

Previous page: *Two ninjas clash on a lonely beach wielding double* **sai** *versus* **katana** *(sword).*
Often rival ninja factions would clash, the outcome determined by the warrior whose skill was supreme.

Below: *Ninja caltrops or* **tetsubishi:** *sharp metal spikes tipped with poison that would be strewn in the path of a pursuing enemy.*

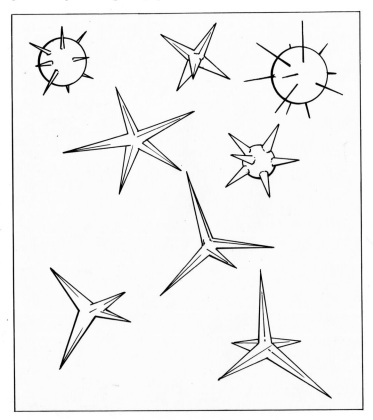

Above: *A female ninja **(kunoichi)** in full battle attack pose, armed with the **shuko** or ninja climbing claw.*

Above right and right: *Ninja **shuko** were lethally effective in close-quarter fighting and equally useful when employed to help scale any awkward object.*

Shuriken – the star-shaped missile

Perhaps the most famous weapon of the ninja was the *shuriken,* the star-shaped missile that could be thrown with deadly accuracy. Although multi-pointed *shuriken* were the type most commonly used, the various ninja clans used other shapes as well, such as the swastika, originally a Sanskrit emblem. Other *shuriken* resembled short darts or knife blades. *Shuriken* were easily concealed in a pocket, but within easy reach if they were needed in an emergency. Because of the mystical overtones in the ninja clans, most field agents carried nine *shuriken* in their pocket, this number being considered lucky.

During childhood training the ninja would have repeatedly thrown the *shuriken* into targets shaped as humans until his accuracy was assured. Aim and timing became almost second nature, and a ninja could throw *shuriken* so fast that it was not unusual actually to have six or seven in the air at the same time.

The *shuriken* is held between the thumb and the forefinger, and thrown in a similar method to that of someone dealing out cards. The razor-sharp pointed objects whizzing through the air would throw even the hardiest of pursuers into a panic. Again the tips of these *shuriken* would no doubt have been coated with some form of poison, so the slightest scratch could mean instant death. The ninja, if disturbed whilst wandering through the darkened chambers of a sleeping castle, could spread panic and confusion by hurling the star-shaped objects into the room. Because *shuriken* were black they would be virtually invisible to the naked eye if hurled into a darkened room. A ninja would always retain at least one *shuriken* upon his person for close-quarter combat. An enemy struggling with a cornered ninja could suddenly find a very sharp *shuriken* placed under his armpit and his arm forced downwards onto the evil points.

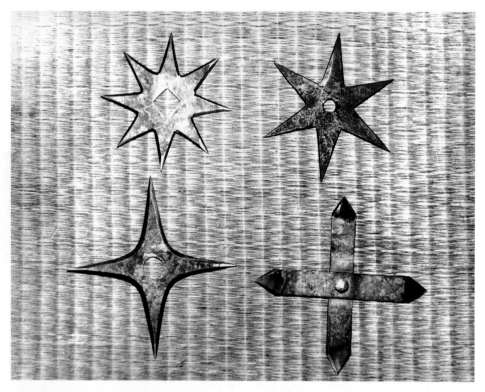

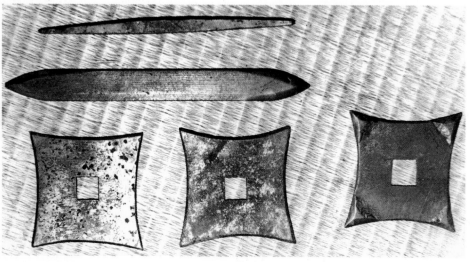

The many varied shapes and sizes of the ninja projectile weapons called **shuriken.** *Although these weapons were designed to be thrown, many were used for stabbing in close-quarter conflicts.*

*Unlike the early weapons used by the ninja of old, **shuriken** today are manufactured from finest quality steel and have razor-sharp points. Note the method used to hurl the **shuriken:** it is placed between two fingers and pulled back across the body before being unleashed.*

Arrows from nowhere

The *yumi* was the ninja bow and arrow, which was carried about in a bamboo tube for protection. This ninja weapon was much shorter than the conventional longbow of the samurai and Japanese troops, which facilitated its easy transportation. The ninja could ambush his designated target with ease from some concealed position. An arrow flying out of nowhere could not be heard or seen – just felt. His aim and accuracy was such that he usually only needed one arrow to accomplish his task.

A lord out hunting with his retainers would suddenly fall from his mount mortally wounded. The hapless samurai could search all day long for the perpetrator, but to no avail. The lone ninja appeared as a ghost in the forest and melted back just as easily, his task accomplished. More than likely the ninja would have burrowed under the earth and then covered himself over with a type of trap door. A small spy hole would have enabled him to see his target approach. Earlier, the ninja most probably spent days taking notes of his target's daily habits, thus establishing a routine. As time was of no consequence to the ninja – only the misson mattered – he could take note of every detail and thus arrange an ambush that had everything in his own favour by way of concealment and escape.

The ninja's ingenuity for adaptation enabled him to make all types of arrows and so create havoc inside enemy positions. Specially-constructed arrows carried messages, bombs, flares, and even ropes so that difficult walls or cliffs could be scaled easily. Sometimes the ninja tipped the point of his arrow with poison, thus making sure that the enemy would die even if he were only wounded. An invading army could soon be put to rout by using a few well-placed ninja with fire and exploding arrows.

Over the many years as technology grew so did the ninja's arsenal. With explosives came the ninja's own home-made mortar. Exploding land-mines, although crudely constructed, were often very effective. Other weapons they carried and used were such items as a flute, which could be converted into a blowpipe for poisonous darts. The *yari* or common spear was adapted to become the *bisento* which is a type of wide-bladed spear.

Walking on water

When looking at the ninja's tools of the trade, weapons constituting just a small part of this category, one cannot help being in awe at the lengths he went to in order to be successful. Legends relate that the ninja could walk on water just like a *kami* spirit. Although this is only part truth, the ninja could actually manage this feat. He was able to ford a river by means of a water-crossing device called a *ukidaru* or floating pot. These were merely waterproof reed pots which the ninja wore on each leg like a huge pair of waders such as trout fishermen wear. Aided by a long bamboo pole the ninja could cross a castle moat or river with relative ease and in this way could keep his explosive powders dry.

The ninja's prowess at swimming great distances and holding his breath underwater for long periods of time has already been described. Thus to the frightened peasants the superstition that ninja could assume the powers of fish and live underwater seemed perfectly reasonable. A feudal Japanese farmer witnessing an escaping ninja dive into a lake or river and not come back up until after the pursuing troops had returned home, was enough to make his blood run cold.

Travelling light

Quite often the ninja's mission involved the penetration of enemy lines and fortifications for purposes of assassination or espionage. Such missions required stealth, speed and unencumbered manoeuvrability. This being the case, the ninja often travelled lightly armed. If he was discovered by a samurai warrior, or rival ninja, he would turn his attacker's weapon back upon him, killing his assailant and then retaining the weapon for his own use.

Finally, one of the most practical weapons the ninja used which was always on hand was a short stick about 3 feet (1 metre) in length called a *hanbo* or half-staff. This stick can be used for striking, throwing and locking techniques.

Previous page: *A ninja battle is ensuing. The simple handle of a rice grinder, called a* **tonfa***, is being utilised as a blocking weapon against the ninja with the staff. Tonfa were used in pairs, just like the ninja's other favourite weapon the* **sai***.*

Right: *At the moment of truth, the more skilled and ruthless ninja emerges victorious. Here the ninja strikes and demolishes his enemy in one fell swoop. After a confrontation such as this, the victor would move his dead adversary away and bury him so that his friends would not discover the body and suspect that a rival ninja was working in their area.*

5

THE NINJA WAY OF LIFE

To learn the true meaning of victory, go and ask the defeated warrior

The art of ninjutsu employs a vast collection of esoteric knowledge that provides the basis for the ninja's unique approach to life and the understanding of it. They, more than any, were at one with their environment. Ninja and the art they so fervently follow is a total way of life in which all aspects of nature and the natural elements, plus man's own consciousness and total perspective of his understanding, are blended together, to provide a life that is at one and in harmony with the universe.

The five elemental manifestations

The Shugendo teachings of the ninja were heavily influenced by many of the East's mystical doctrines, incorporating into their realm such treatises as the Tao Te Ching, I Ching, and the Tantric beliefs of Tibet, plus of course Buddhism. These, and other forms of mysticism, were used in experiencing and interpreting the will and flow of the universe. Ninjutsu tactics and techniques often incorporate the symbolism of nature to provide inspiration for practical application. Within the philosophy of ninjutsu are incorporated what are known as the Go Dai, the five elemental manifestations, the progression of which are: Ku=Void, Fu=Wind, Ka=Fire, Sui=Water, Chi=Earth.

This progression depicts the creation of the universe and symbolises the ways that physical matter manifests itself as formless combustive energy creating in its turn energy, liquids, solids and gas. From this come what are termed the Go Gyo, or five prime elements which describe how things interrelate and operate, much like the Chinese *yin* and *yang*. These elements are: Chi=Earth, Sui=Water, Ka=Fire, Moku=Wood, Kin=Metal.

Continuously working, these elements interact to create and then destroy each other. Water feeds the growing tree, which is then felled by the metal axe, and then consumed by the fire to finally scatter into ashes on the earth. The ninja align these five principals so that they can be seen as they operate in the regulation of an individual's health and also in the unfolding of life's events.

The ninja's Taoist heritage, taken from Chinese teachings over a thousand years before, brought about a familiarity with nature, and natural laws became the theory behind the application of ninjutsu escape skills. The skill of tonjutsu, the earth methods, involved the use of rocks, soil and land contours to aid the ninja in his escape. Sui tonjutsu, or water methods, involve the use of special equipment for moving across the surface of ponds, rivers, swamps, moats and lakes, as well as utilizing unique techniques and apparatus for remaining submerged under water for long periods.

Invoking the kuji power principle

One of the most misunderstood aspects of ninjutsu by non-practitioners of the art is the ninja concept of *kuji*. *Kuji* means 'nine syllables' and it is one of the exotic and sometimes thought of as bizarre skills of the ancient ninja warriors. By weaving their fingers together in what seems to resemble something of a Gordian knot, and at the same time mumbling an obscure incantation, the ninja could perform the most impossible task that would make mere mortals cringe. Legends relate that the ninja walked across water, disappeared like ghosts, flew through the air like demons, and were invisible to humans. The truth behind these stories arises from ninja applying the *kuji* principles of mind and body in total harmony and their ability to adapt to any given situation. In reality, the *kuji* power principle stems from the ancient mystical teachings of northern India and Tibet. These were brought to Japan during China's T'ang dynasty (AD 618-907) and formed part of the esoteric lore that later came to be known as Mikkyo or the secret doctrines.

Today's ninja practitioners and students, after adopting the standard ninja training syllabus, go on to learn the higher order of the ninja art which they term Ninpo. Ninpo reflects the nature of the art and the needs that caused it to come into being. The *kuji* hand-weaving configurations are, in actuality, only one-third of the whole of the *kuji* concept. They represent the physical body in action, which must then be joined by the intellect and the will in order to produce the desired results.

The three elements of thought, word and deed, are co-ordinated and attuned with each other to make up the ninja's *kuji* power principle. This system is, in reality, a method of learning to remove the gap that separates intention from successful action. The rational mind, having its own limitations, can refuse subconsciously to attempt anything that seems impossible. But by overriding this natural process anything and everything becomes possible to the ninja, who at the same time still retains the feasibility choice. Or in other words by invoking the *kuji* power principle, the user begins not only to believe he can apply himself towards an endeavour, but also knows that it will be

a success without endangering himself. Once the *kuji* technique is mastered the ninja then has the power to create physical reality by means of his intention alone. Focused intention becomes completed action itself: cause blends with effect until the distinction fades.

The mind as a weapon

Invoking *kuji* power in a combat application allows the ninja the ability to focus his intention to gain power or energy that seems to defy normal physical laws. This intention-focusing does not actually create extra energy, but rather removes the limits that usually restrict the amount of energy available to the normal individual. This concept is much similar to the adepts of yoga, who by focusing their mind and will are able to perform seemingly extraordinary feats that defy explanation. Advanced mystical techniques such as this gave the illusion to the uninitiated that the invoker possessed great magical power – and where ignorance abounds legends begin.

A common misconception about this higher order of the art is that ninjutsu followers put themselves in danger by adopting the *kuji* methods of trance-like action. This is totally wrong. The physical body is capable of performing the techniques; the mind understands what has to be done; and the will is unhesitating and determines that the task will be completed successfully.

The mind as a weapon can be truely awesome if applied to the right area of circumstances. None knew this better than the ninja himself: basic and advanced psychology were important lessons that the ninja learned thoroughly if he was to stay alive. Every advantage was an edge. The ninja saw the average person as having five basic weaknesses, which he categorized as Fear, Sympathy, Vanity, Anger and Laziness. He found the greatest weapon was exploiting one of these weaknesses. Some adversaries almost always react in the same manner and can be identified with one specific weakness above all others, but others fluctuate from one weakness to another, depending on the circumstances. By capitalizing on an adversary's emotional weakness, the ninja could manipulate his target's fundamental needs.

In an espionage manoeuvre a ninja agent, by catering to or supplying a need, could develop a feeling of obligation in the person being cultivated. Later, this debt could be touched upon when the ninja needed assistance or some item of information. Again the ninja classified these basic needs into five broad categories: Security, Sex, Wealth, Pride and Pleasure.

Above left: *The eight trigrams which form the basis for the Chinese book of divination called the **I-Ching**. These eight trigrams all have an attribute which can be further broken down into 64 hexagrams. Seen in the centre is the symbol known as the **yin-yang** which always indicates the continuous flowing force of the universe, which the ninja tapped into during their meditative moment when channelling energy.*

Left: *Taijutsu teaches confidence – even when you are up against a much larger and heavier opponent.*

Right: *Nagato **sensei** adopts the pose known as **ichimonji**, which is one of the basic positions of taijutsu.*

Previous page: *Stephen Hayes of the USA with a **bo** staff. The power that the **bo** could generate in an attack was quite devastating. The tip of the staff, with the ninja's concentrated force behind it, was capable of penetrating the heavy armour of the samurai.*

Above: *Nagato* **sensei** *executing movements from the ninja body art of taijutsu. In an attack situation only the very slightest movement is needed in order for the defender to repel an oncoming attack. The Chinese have an expression which perhaps exemplifies this concept: 'Deviate an inch and lose a thousand miles.'*

Previous page: *A group of ninja spring out of the darkness of the forest. The lead ninja holds his sword aloft ready to do battle. His cohorts keep back to size up the situation and if necessary they will leap into action also.*

Left: *A ninja practitioner adopts the ready position of* **ichimonji** *in defence of an impending attack. He then delivers a low kick in retaliation. The ninja kick resembles more of a stomp than a straight kick, as in other martial arts.*

Ninja mind games

The ninja agent, also a mere mortal, could fall into his own trap of self-desires. If a need arose within the ninja's own personality, such as pride, pleasure or even wealth – the weaknesses he was taught to look out for in others – then he could be caught in the 'needs' trap. The ninja's key to overcoming this problem in his mental make-up was for him mentally to run through a kind of self-examination programme. In this mind game, he examined his own needs and wants, and then openly and honestly evaluated them, judged them for what they were and then cast them aside. In knowing himself, the ninja could come to an honest appraisal of his weaknesses and those areas where he was vulnerable. After reaching this point, the ninja would then find ways of strengthening the potential trouble areas in his own egotistical make-up. The ninja agent could not allow any kind of self-weakness to mar his thinking and thus make him weak. He could not just close his eyes and pretend the weakness did not exist. Ultimately he had to satisfy his needs through personal understanding, and eventually work the weaknesses out of his personality.

This brilliant ability for self-analysis could take him to the stage where he could totally overcome most basic inherent human traits, to arrive at the position whereby he could actually conquer the ego itself. Incredible as it may sound, the ninja's mental ability was such that he could be put on a par with today's practising psychologists. This inestimable power of catering to a person's inner wants and needs gave the ninja a very powerful weapon indeed. The *kunoichi* (female ninja) perhaps excelled in these abilities more so than their male counterparts.

Left: *A **kunoichi** conceals herself behind a tree trunk with sword drawn. A single-hand slashing thrust from this position was used primarily for attacking the soft fleshy areas of the enemy's body, as little strength was required in order to inflict the maximum amount of damage.*

Right: *Since the **kunoichi** were trained musicians it would not be unusual for them to be seen with a flute – which could be converted into a poisonous-dart blow gun if necessary.*

The fearless ones

A famous ninja escapade involved the ninja folk hero Goemon. In fact, the plot of this legend is so fascinating that hundreds of years later it was used for a sequence in the James Bond movie *You Only Live Twice*. The story relates that Goemon was sent to kill the notorious Oda Nobunaga. After great difficulties in gaining entrance to his castle (it is said Goemon waited over two months in the area) he finally succeeded in entering and quickly made his way to Nobunaga's sleeping quarters, which to his dismay were completely surrounded by his samurai bodyguard. Using his imaginative powers, Goemon crawled along the precarious rafters above the ceiling and entered a small attic above the lord's bedchamber. Next he drilled a small hole into the ceiling right in line with Nobunaga's futon (bed). When the lord retired for the night, Goemon waited until the man was fast asleep. Then noiselessly he lowered a thin silk strand until it hung suspended just above the lips of his sleeping victim. Taking out a small phial of deadly poison from his concealed pouch he proceeded to spill a drop at a time down the long silken thread. As the deadly fluid was inches away from the lips of Nobunaga, the lord turned suddenly to his side and awoke just in time to see what was happening. Goemon had to make a run for his life and barely escaped. Before this intrepid ninja had another chance to fulfil his mission the evil Nobunaga was slain at the hands of someone else.

Such was the importance of the ninja's mission that even his own death was of little consequence – as long as he was successful. The ninja's outlook towards death was about the only thing that they had in common with the samurai. To both warrior castes death held no fear – it was just an occurrence. Over the centuries the myth of the ninja has grown, along with folklore and fiction. But one thing above all else is certain: the ninja warrior was a force to be reckoned with.

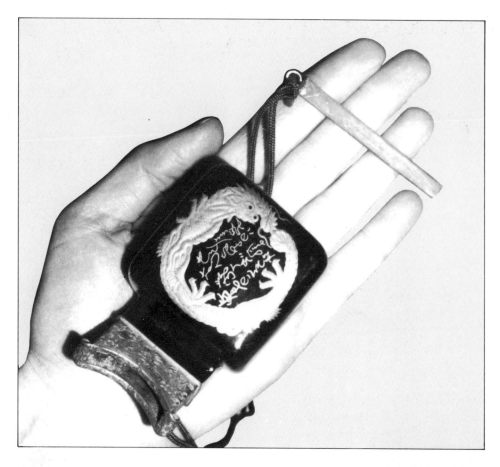

Left: *This unique box, containing dust, was used by the ninja. When blown into, it emitted a fine dust screen to blind an attacker.*

Right and below: *The female ninja would use all her feminine charms and stoop to any unorthodox methods in order to fulfil her mission. Once the intended victim was beguiled the **kunoichi**'s flashing dagger would be produced from out of her tunic and the death of the victim would result.*

Petals of death

In another tale a certain ninja was sent out to kill the lord of Nagoya castle. But no matter how hard he tried the ninja just couldn't get near his target's private apartments. The lord's defences were such that he did not venture anywhere without a huge retinue of personal samurai. Even when he slept, six samurai were in the bed chamber, working on a rota of three awake and three asleep. Such security the ninja had never experienced before. The ninja knew he could not return unsuccessful, so some other method had to be devised. Week after week went by and the ninja kept a close watch on his target, looking for even the slightest break or alteration in the lord's routine that would give him the opportunity to make his move. From a vantage point deep in the foliage of a large tree the ninja watched the lord perform all his daily duties. He noticed that each morning and evening the lord took a stroll around his well-kept garden and seemed to pay particular attention to a huge rose bush. Without fail, every day the lord would stoop to smell each rose on the bush before returning to his duties.

So the ninja hit upon a plan. In the late afternoon he sneaked into the garden and coated each rose with a deadly but sweet-smelling poison that once inhaled would bring instant death. At dusk, the lord made the usual rounds of his adored garden. As he stooped to smell the delicate perfume of the rose, he inhaled the deadly fumes and seconds later fell to the ground clutching at his throat. In a moment he was dead. The ninja had accomplished what he had been sent out to do, and escaped silently into the night.

*Leading **sensei** of the world of ninjutsu, Nagato, Hatsumi, and Doron Novon, at Europe's largest ninja training camp, called a **tai-kai**.*

6

NINJA UNARMED COMBAT SKILLS

**Those who talk least hear
the most**

Although the ninja warrior was a walking arsenal, there were times when he could be caught without any weapon at all. It was on these occasions that to defend himself he had to rely on unarmed combat skills called taijutsu, which literally translated means 'body art'. Taijutsu forms the basis for all understanding in the fighting arts of ninjutsu.

Bonds of brotherhood

In today's martial arts it is taijutsu that is taught to prospective ninja students. Unlike the martial arts skills of karate, taekwondo, etc, which are for the most part very competition orientated, ninjutsu offers a complete self-protection programme.

The atmosphere in a ninja training hall promotes bonds of brotherhood, rather than students being in direct competition with one another and it is interesting that this approach is common all around the world in ninja training today. Many beginners, who come into ninjutsu training from other martial arts, often remark that they can feel and sense this friendly effusive air that pervades. The centre of all ninja training is located in Japan under the direct guidance of the art's grandmaster Dr Masaaki Hatsumi, who is the 34th grandmaster of the Togakure Ryu Ninja.

The four fighting positions

Taijutsu is unlike any other empty-hand Japanese system. Taijutsu stresses body dynamics, the principle of using the whole of the body as a weapon. There is no basic fighting stance, which is always determined by the relationship of the fighter to his opponent. However, although this may appear to be something of a contradiction, there are actually four main fighting positions, but these are only used as a framework for the student so that he can gain an understanding of how taijutsu operates.

These four fighting positions consist of the natural stance, defensive stance, offensive stance and receiving stance. This last stance seems, at first glance, to have similarities with the aikido principle, which makes use of evasion and then countering. It is sometimes interpreted as inviting an attack, or misinterpreted as surrendering to one. This is because the practitioner stands in a relaxed manner with his arms and legs spread wide open, as though he were about to give in. As the attack commences, the taijutsu exponent appears to vanish, but then suddenly rises up behind the attacker, to mete out his own justice.

Because taijutsu is strictly a combat martial art, the aim of its proponents is to inflict the greatest possible damage with the fewest moves and easiest methods. The art encompasses grappling, throws and escapes, locks, chokes, and muscle and bone attacks. All the time the student has to control the fight – once control is lost, so too is the fight itself.

The key to this efficient and effective movement is co-ordinated rhythm. For obvious reasons any encounter is a spontaneous and sudden action, requiring a response without even thinking. To enable the ninja student to train for this, special exercises were devised to act as a foundation. These are sparring, target-hitting, shadow boxing, and visualization. The first three are self-explanatory. The fourth, visualization, is employed to

Previous page: *Grandmaster Masaaki Hatsumi strikes up an attack pose from the repertoire of taijutsu. Any hand manoeuvre is not a committed movement. The master adopts an eye-gouging pose, which can be converted instantly into an open-palm strike.*

Stephen Hayes demonstrating the rudiments of the ninja stomping kick. In this kick the leg is never really fully extended upon impact. The kick resembles a stomp, in which most of the power is delivered by the heel.

increase the student's awareness so he can assimilate the principles of various body movements. The aim is to visualize in the training hall the effects of certain attacks and counters under controlled conditions, thereby training the conciousness to develop a kind of sixth sense. The concept is that the student reads a situation before it happens, then he can never be surprised by an attack.

Anticipating the unexpected

Beginners start by learning to block and counter, but by the time the student gets to a higher grade his actions depend on where he happens to be at that particular time in body-positioning terms during a fight. When a student throws an adversary he never really knows where or how he is going to land. In taijutsu terms, the student can't determine the next move by stating he has to execute this particular armlock, or that particular hold. So in training students are given lots of exercises that involve moving from side to side in rapid succession. This develops a feeling of how an opponent will move or react when grabbed. This knowledge is then logged and students train repeatedly so that both movement and reaction become instinctual.

As training progresses some light sparring is introduced, but again it is pretty much a case of 'anything goes'. Kicks and strikes are delivered at a distance, then when the distance gap is closed, armlocks and short-range strikes are implemented. The instructor instils into the students that when they are sparring, it's not a 'win at all costs' situation but that they have to learn to take one or two knocks themselves, just to experience the feeling of being hit. Then in a life-or-death situation, the feeling of being hit won't come as too much of a shock and therefore distract them, thus allowing it to become a weakness. In early training elaborate balancing manoeuvres are taught, which involve a light form of gymnastics. Students learn how to perform handstands whilst someone holds their legs. Movement, or more correctly body movement, is the key that unlocks ninjutsu's many techniques.

Below: *Grandmaster Hatsumi executing a side-stepping block . As the attacker strikes the* **sensei** *moves quickly forwards, thus cutting down the distance and also halving the attacker's power.*

Left: *Dave Evans of England adopts a taijutsu stance. His whole body is prepared and ready to meet any kind of imminent attack. His foot can strike out as can his hands, thus defeating an adversary before he has a chance to do any damage.*

Right: *Stephen Hayes in the final stages of defeating an opponent. The enemy is trapped on the ground between his legs thus preventing any kind of retaliatory attack.*

A continuous flowing motion

Apart from the four fighting positions previously mentioned, part of the platform from which students begin is introduced as the front stance *(ju mongi no kamae)* and the back stance *(ichi mongi no kamae)*. Using these two very basic stances the student is taken through a set series of 18 techniques called 'kamae no kata'. This sequence of movement teaches the student to flow from one position to another, and yet again into another and so on, but in a continuous smooth motion. The kamae no kata encompasses the basic techniques that a student first experiences in taijutsu unarmed combat training and it aids the beginner in linking up movements before he becomes adept at actually falling into an instinctive reactionary role from which to operate. It teaches the student to flow from left to right and assume fighting platforms or stances from which to execute attacks and counters. Using this set training programme allows the ninja student to further his training when he or she is not under the direct supervision of the instructor.

The basic techniques *(kihon happo)* in taijutsu consist of three punching techniques, three one-handed grabs, and two two-handed grabs. Students perform these movements in pairs and they don't practise as though one side was trying to catch the other. They perform the techniques close

up and are encouraged to help one another – thus maintaining the brotherhood of the art. The idea is to get the techniques to flow. Once the flow is perfected by the students, then they start to vary the techniques.

Throughout training it is emphasized that the student has to understand body manoeuvrability. Constant training brings an awareness to each student that a given course of action from an opponent can be easily evaded merely by moving their own body out of the way. So subtle is this art of taijutsu, that not even a block is needed to counter an attack from an adversary. Just by moving one way or another, repeated attacks can be stopped without the ninja student ever having to retaliate if they do not wish to.

Left: *By stepping forwards to meet the oncoming sword attack, Hatsumi* **sensei** *nullifies it in an instant. His forward leading arm bar blocks the attacker's downward strike, and at the same time leaves the attacker wide open for a full frontal body strike.*

Below: *Stephen Hayes delivers a counterblow to the inside of his attacker's arm. This strike will not only halt the impending blow but also destroy the arm muscle and thus prevent the adversary from further antagonistic action.*

*Hatsumi **sensei**, by employing a taijutsu leverage motion, finds little difficulty in throwing an opponent to the ground.*

Sensitivity awareness

Involved in taijutsu training are rolling techniques with breakfalls similar to those employed in judo. Cartwheels are another of the ninja's evasion body techniques, which when put into practise during an affray look quite amusing. One popular exercise that helps put a beginner in touch with his or her own body is blindfolded pushing. This involves a student being blindfolded and then having another student push them over. The person blindfolded has no idea from which direction the push is to be initiated, so it comes as a surprise. They then have to breakfall, roll over and come back up assuming a fighting position. As soon as the blindfolded person feels the 'contact' of the other person's body (their hands) pushing them, in an instant they go with it, riding the push and rolling to spring out of it lightly back on their feet. Repetitive training in this area gets the person used to feeling any kind of aggressive pressure from another quarter upon his own person. This type of training teaches balance and sensitivity awareness. Knowing what is going on around you, whether you can see or not, is all part and parcel of the ninja perception technique.

*UK ninja **sensei** Peter King halts a running forwards attack by delivering a palm strike to the opponent's chin and then follows through with a deft body manoeuvre to hurl his adversary to the ground.*

*An attack with a **bokken**. Left: the attacker rushes in to deliver an overhead downward strike. Below: the defender waits until the last moment and calmly steps to the side, the bokken missing its intended target. Right above: The victim now becomes the attacker and loops his arm around his attacker's neck. Right below: He suddenly pulls upwards with his hand and wraps his open palm around his attacker's jaw.*

Far left: *Stephen Hayes adopts the classical ninja back sword draw position. The ninja always carried his sword strapped to his back for easy transportation and to prevent it from being too cumbersome when running.*

Left: *The* **manrikigusari***, the chain weapon of the ninja, is used here to ensnare an unsuspecting sentry.*

The first level of learning

In the body art of taijutsu students have to be brought up to certain fitness levels before they become capable of initiating techniques. Therefore much of the early part of the instructional programme is spent in getting the beginner's body exercised and trained. The principal thinking behind this is that students vary from young to old, and everyone has a different physically active state of fitness. So movement and more movement is involved, aided by circuit training and exercises.

The student's first impressions are that taijutsu is a little like a jigsaw. But over the months and years of training it all begins to slot together, so that when a student arrives at the stage when he takes his proficiency examination, termed *shodan* or black belt, an overall picture of the art of taijutsu has begun to emerge. But even after a student reaches the black belt stage of competency, he has reached only the first level of learning. It can be equated with a driving test: passing your test doesn't make you an expert driver.

Many of the popular martial arts training systems attempt to mould the student's ways of reacting and moving to fit a stylized set of predetermined movements. Taijutsu works in the opposite manner by getting rid of the awkward or unnatural tendencies that may have been picked up unwittingly over the years and concentrating on natural movement. As a fighting system, taijutsu relies on natural body strength and resiliency, speed of response and movement and an understanding of the principles of nature for successful results in self-protection. Taijutsu techniques take advantage of natural physical construction and efficient employment of body dynamics. Although most of these underlying theories are predominantly Chinese in origin (which recent research and discoveries have proven), many distinct subtle changes have been made along the way. For instance, unlike many kung-fu styles, students of taijutsu need not imitate kinds of animals or distort or deform their body structure to employ the techniques. It is interesting to note that the principles behind the body mechanics of taijutsu also provide the foundation for combat with the weapon arts of ninjutsu.

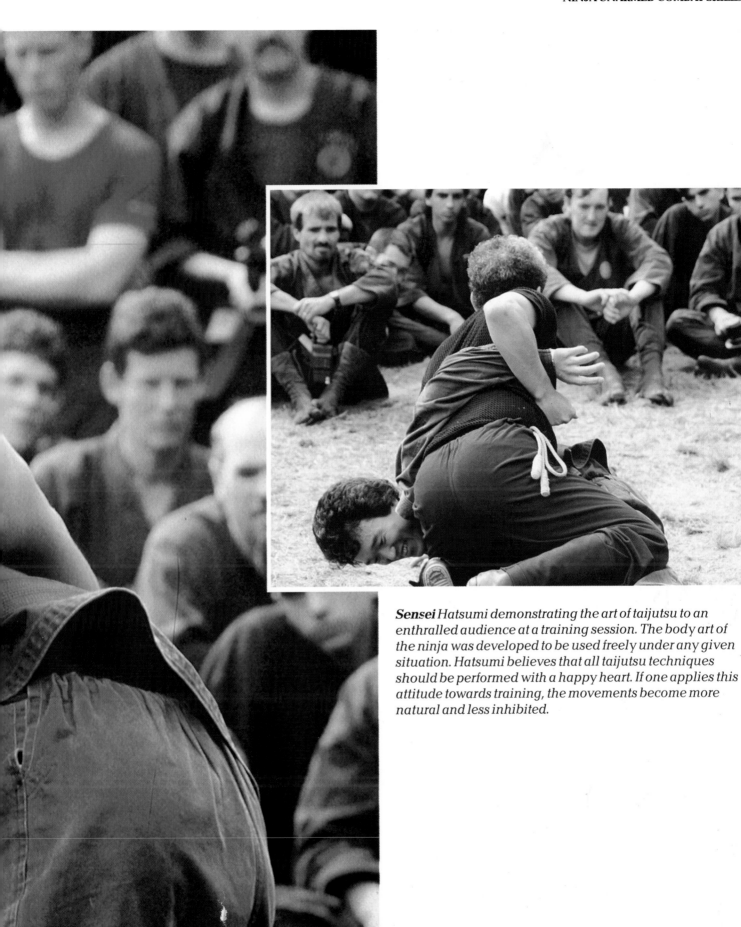

Sensei Hatsumi demonstrating the art of taijutsu to an enthralled audience at a training session. The body art of the ninja was developed to be used freely under any given situation. Hatsumi believes that all taijutsu techniques should be performed with a happy heart. If one applies this attitude towards training, the movements become more natural and less inhibited.

Strength through flexibility

Another integral component of taijutsu is called *junan taiso* or body conditioning. The exercises within this framework contribute to the suppleness, speed and responsive action necessary for the effective application of taijutsu techniques. In training, strength is generated through flexibility. The muscles and joints are exercised to enhance their natural elastic qualities, and not to stretch, strain or tear, as is seen in many other martial arts disciplines. *Junan taiso*'s basic exercise plan institutes a correct and balanced diet which ultimately provides for strength, flexibility and health in general – another indication that the original system has all the hallmarks of being Chinese.

During the practice of the *junan taiso* exercises, it can be observed that the body tissue, fluid circulation, breathing patterns, and active direction of the conciousness are all in harmony with each other. By learning the effects and influences of the body's many maintenance systems, the student of ninjutsu can develop a working knowledge of his or her own power, to control the health and condition of the body.

When attacked, the ninja fights from his basic position – called *ichimonji*. This pose is assumed as the body slides back away from the attack. The back leg carries most of the weight and the leading leg holds the body upright. The shoulders are held low and relaxed with the hands in the open-palm position protecting the face and body. Specific ninja taijutsu techniques number in their thousands and include countless variations on a given theme. Ninja students are not obviously expected to learn all of these, but rather work on internalizing the principles embodied by the techniques.

Right: *The 34th grandmaster of the Togakure ninjutsu system, Dr Masaaki Hatsumi, assumes a ninja taijutsu defence stance. Almost all the ninjutsu taught today involves full use and knowledge of the ninja's self-defence and body art. The few basic stances are only a platform from which to launch many thousands of varied and devastating techniques.*

*The ninja **hanbo** is the first weapon a modern-day ninjutsu practitioner learns to handle. Although only a simple stick, many hundreds of different movements, involving strikes, locks and slashes, can be permutated within the sphere of **hanbo** techniques.*

*The student rushes in with an overhead attack with a **hanbo**. As the weapon comes crashing in, a simple side-stepping manoeuvre by Hatsumi **sensei** puts him instantly out of harm's way. Fear of a weapon can seriously impair a defender's judgement and reaction to an attack, thus an intensive mind-training programme is part of the ninjutsu training method.*

Handling any situation

Spontaneity, or automatically reacting with the responding appropriate action to the elements of the circumstances, is a crucial skill for self-defence. The ninja student is prepared to adapt to any situation that confronts him and is not tempted to force the situation to fit the parameters of some specialized training system – which again highlights the differences between ninjutsu and other popular martial arts. The broad scope of ninja training has therefore evolved to include methods to handle any situation. The martial arts student who is only trained to punch will encounter great difficulty in situations where his punching skills are ineffective or inappropriate. True proficiency in self-defence comes from a blending of all areas of skill with the body, and cannot result from the dangerous and limiting concept of developing a speciality, which if it fails leaves the person wide open to counter-movements from an aggressor.

The body knows how to move if we let it and does not require active 'mental control to respond properly in a threatening situation. The student of taijutsu works to eliminate the awkward process of first mechanically thinking through a response before actually carrying it out.

Ninjutsu's natural stance involves quite simply standing in a relaxed manner with the arms loosely hanging down by the sides. The knees are straight but not locked back. This position employs the ninja earth principle. The second stance is the defensive posture, which is used to counter the opponent's techniques. The emphasis on this posture is to let the hips move first, with the body following. This posture employs the ninja water principle of being fluid. The third position is the offensive posture, best described as slightly similar to that of a boxer's stance. The ninja in this position moves forward to meet his attacker, the power coming from the trunk of the body and not the shoulders. The fire element is this position's principle. The last posture is the receiving stance. In this amazing position the ninja quite literally stands spreadeagled, arms and legs spread wide apart, looking foolishly open to any attack under the sun. But, like the art it belongs to, this position is very deceiving. Based on the ninja principle of the wind, this receiving pose makes use of evasion.

Dr Masaaki Hatsumi **sensei** and a leading Western exponent of ninjutsu, Doron Novon of Israel, demonstrating ninja swordplay. Novon as the attacker steps forwards and strikes downwards. Hatsumi **sensei** sidesteps and at the same time blocks the striking arm. He then brings his lead hand forwards and pulls down on the dull edge of the sword. Then palming the blade, he traps Novon's hands, thereby preventing him from any further attack.

Awarding progress

All training in taijutsu is practised in a standard black suit. Examinations are taken at varying intervals to judge and assess the student's progress in the system and the knowledge he or she has accumulated during training. Coloured belts are awarded (as is usual in all Japanese martial arts) when a student is successful in passing the set test. All beginners start off with a white belt, which ultimately leads to the *shodan* or black belt. Along the way there are nine stages to be completed. The first grade is termed *kyu* and is identified by a green belt, which is superseded as proficiency increases by the next grade downwards, e.g. 8th, 7th, 6th, etc.

In ninjutsu the green coloured belt never changes until the student becomes a black belt, unlike in other Japanese martial arts where the colours change according to grade.

To identify the degrees of proficiency of the lower grades a star is awarded which is then sewn on to the official badge of the organization. These stars are silver and each grade passed adds another to the badge until the student has four, which will then make him a 4th *kyu*. From this stage the star colour changes to gold, four of these stars being required for the student to take his black belt examination and consequently become an instructor himself – although the learning of the art continues for a lifetime.

All *kyu* grades wear a badge with the Japanese calligraphy for ninjutsu emblazoned upon it in white on a red background with a white border. The *dan* or black belt badge carries black calligraphy on a red background with a white border. Taijutsu's grading system, the same all over the world, was instituted at the Japanese headquarters of grandmaster Dr Masaaki Hatsumi.

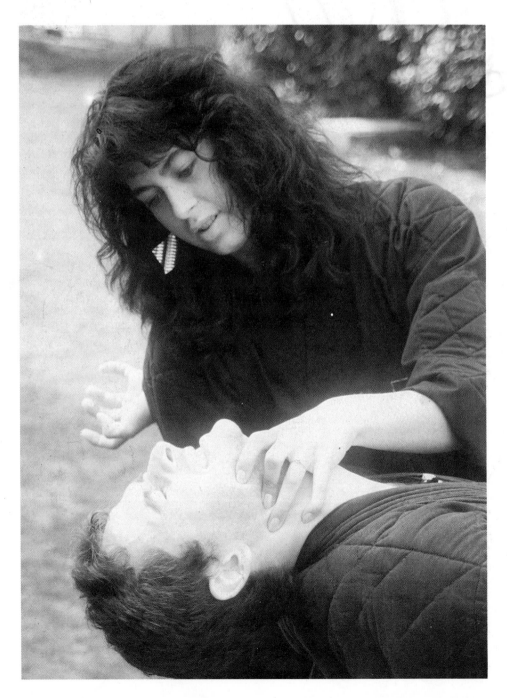

*The **kunoichi** was an expert with chain weapons as well as the unarmed combat art of taijutsu. **Manrikusari** in expert hands was an extremely versatile weapon. It could be used to block an attack and then be converted into an attack weapon itself.*

Grandmaster of ninjutsu Dr Masaaki Hatsumi demonstrating classic strike positions with the ninja sword. The short blade of the ninja sword allowed a great deal of manoeuvrability and versatility. The blade of the samurai sword was much longer and heavier.

THE MODERN-DAY NINJA

7

The highest branch is not always the safest roost

As the twentieth century winds towards its close, the world's global community is witnessing more and more chaos – both in society and at the very roots of its government. International terrorism is rife, assassination, both political and personal, is commonplace. The world's military and law-enforcement agencies are having to recruit and train specialized personnel who are best equipped to deal with the worsening situation. These elite groups of fighters or security forces are delving into the past for their training methods in an effort to combat and neutralize the destructive elements that exist in our society.

Bloody showdown in London

Much of the advanced training is obviously very secret, but one wonders if the ancient art of ninjutsu is still very much alive and kicking in the special service units secret training camps, creating a type of modern ninja armed with the very latest technological weapons and forming the super-ninja units of tomorrow.

The art of ninjutsu is a system encompassing almost limitless conflict techniques and weaponry principles which can be adapted to almost any clandestine conflict anywhere in the world – from the deserts of Saudi Arabia to Central American jungle camps. In the United States Defense Department analysts have studied ninjutsu techniques and history to such an extent that they have evolved a tactical treatise based upon the art of the ancient ninja. In Great Britain not too long ago an incident sparked off a political storm that ultimately led to an assault on the

Iranian embassy in London in an attempt to free hostages that were being held against their will. The elite paramilitary unit known as the SAS were sent in to relieve the situation. Suddenly the world's TV screens were filled with black-masked figures spewing out of low-flying helicopters, sliding down ropes and crashing through plate-glass windows to rescue the hostages in a bloody showdown. For all the world, without the technology, they could have been a ninja clan from out of Japan's feudal past once again plying their trade with deadly efficiency.

The art of winning

From elitist military groups to the ordinary individual, the man in the street, ninjutsu is an ancient art that can be employed as a means for individual defence and survival in our modern world. In fact, it has become more than just a martial art: its development through the ages has reached the point where the art actually embraces life itself. The city executive or businessman about to embark on a deal – all can gain something from the qualities that ninjutsu has to offer. As the Western authority on the system Shidoshi Stephen Hayes once said, 'Ninjutsu is the art of winning'.

Built within the modern framework of teaching, the art no longer instructs its adepts to skulk around in the dead of night, but allows the student, no matter what the circumstances, freely to interpret the techniques and use them accordingly, whether they apply to body manoeuvres (taijutsu) in a street self-defence situation, or to the psychological aspects of the art in a boardroom battle.

NINJA THUNDERBOLT

COLOUR. 90 MINS.

NT 012

VHS

18

His Blood is motivated
by the Ninja Spirit,
and a Ninja must
succeed or die...

NINJA THUNDERBOLT

THE DEADLY WARRIOR,
THE MOST POWERFUL FORCE

18

RICHARD HARRISON
NINJA THUNDERBOLT
WANG TAO   ANNA LEWIS   JACKIE CHAN
RANDY TO   KULADA YASUAKI   BARBARA YUEN

Previous page: The picture that shook the world: modern-day contemporaries of the ancient ninja warriors in action. The British special unit known as the SAS crashing through the windows of the Iranian embassy in London to break the siege, after first abseiling out of low-flying helicopters.

These and following pages: Typical of the ninja mania that appears to be sweeping the world, the current boom in ninja movies and videos is indicative of the popularity in this ancient warrior art to the modern youth of today.

Movie superheroes

The current trends in ninjutsu ensure that the art of the ninja is going to be with us for a long time into the future. Hollywood, through the celluloid image, is perpetuating the lifestyle of these shadow warriors and in true movie-maker's tradition is depicting them as superheroes transposed from Japan's dark feudal past into the present day. With video films being released almost monthly about ninja, the word 'ninjamania' has suddenly crept into our vocabulary. The television industry was quick to follow suit and produced a series called 'The Master', starring Lee van Cleef. Almost overnight the name ninja has become a household word, just as kung-fu became back in the early seventies when the late Bruce Lee burst onto the scene.

It is interesting to note that, apart from the many students who train in the martial art of ninjutsu around the world, there exists a quite separate group of individuals who can be termed 'ninja enthusiasts'. These devotees, however, are not interested in learning the ancient skills of the art, but merely follow the ways of the ninja by donning black uniforms and face masks and acting out in the privacy of their own homes some of the escapades of the *shinobi* warriors.

Some martial artists have taken to the acting profession and people such as Chuck Norris *(The Octagon)* and Sho Kosugi, who made such movies as *Nine Deaths of the Ninja, Ninja 3 the Domination* and *Revenge of the Ninja*, have became overnight stars. The box office success of these films assured the Hollywood producers that the subject of ninja was big business. More recently a relatively unknown star named David Dudikoff has had a huge box office hit with the film *American Ninja*.

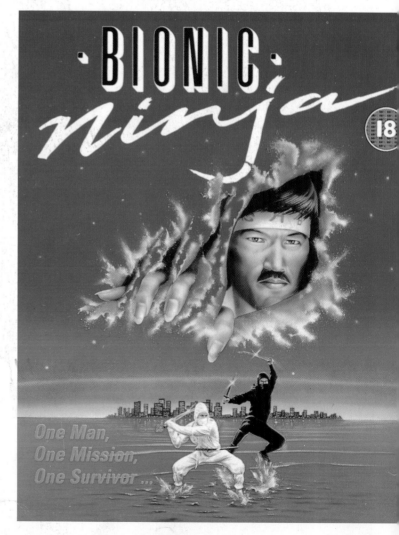

BIONIC ninja

18

One Man,
One Mission,
One Survivor ...

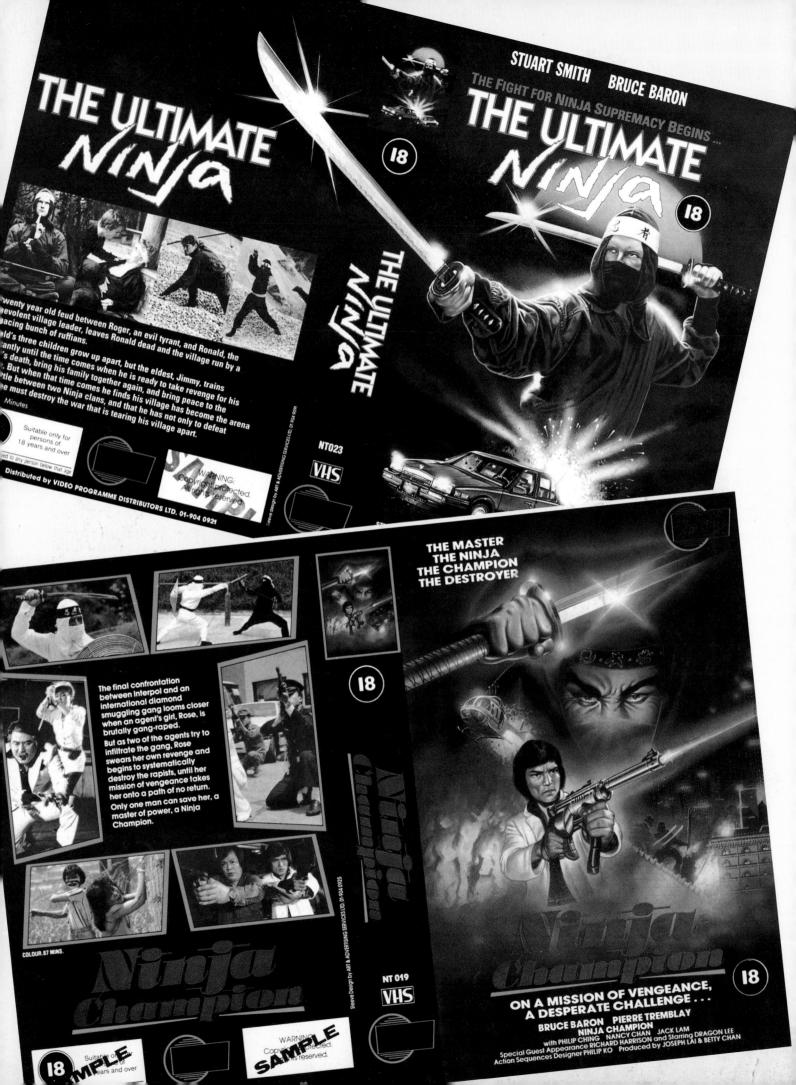

SHO KOSUGI in **the Mas...**

starrin...

LEE ...
and ...

RICHARD HARRISON **STUART SMITH** in

COBRA AGAINST NINJA

The grandmaster's successor

But what has happened to the ninja in Japan? Most of the ninjutsu taught in the world today emanates from a quiet suburb of Noda City in Chiba prefecture. It is here that the present grandmaster of the art, Dr Masaaki Hatsumi, has his *dojo* (school). Hatsumi *sensei* (teacher) is a bone-setter by profession but a ninjutsu teacher *par excellence* by succession. The title of grandmaster was bestowed upon him by the late 33rd grandmaster and Hatsumi's own instructor, *sensei* Toshitsugu Takamatsu. Until that time (1972) no Westerner has ever been taught the art. In fact Hatsumi *sensei* in his earlier days used to train in ninjutsu dressed in a white suit similar to those used in karate and judo, just to disguise what he was practising. Toshitsugu Takamatsu was totally against anyone other than a Japanese learning the art. So, in effect, Dr Hatsumi broke with tradition slightly when he opened up instruction to Europeans and Americans.

Ninja tradition dictates that even now Dr Hatsumi will be looking for a successor to become the 35th grandmaster. It is a long process of knowing and learning, and finding a person with the suitable qualities required to assume leadership. If, by chance, he cannot find an heir, he will destroy all his scrolls and his own personal ninja weapons. He will leave nothing behind him. This is the strict clan code and system, which dates back nearly 800 years to the first founder of the ninja Togakure system, *soke* Daisuke Togakure, the Japanese word *soke* meaning founder of a school or system. If and when Dr Hatsumi finds a successor from amongst his many worldwide schools, that person will be unaware of his future role. But unbeknown to him he will be groomed in the ninja ways and traditions and singled out for special skills training. He will learn all that is required to become, one day, the 35th grandmaster of ninjutsu.

Left: Hatsumi **sensei** instructing a ninja student in the art of finger jabbing.

Right: Hatsumi and Nagato **sensei** enjoy a free sparring session in their younger days. Here Hatsumi **sensei** attempts to pull Nagato **sensei** over with a taijutsu arm-locking manoeuvre.

Survive or die

The modern world has spawned another application for the ninja arts. With the threat of global nuclear war hanging over us like a Damaclesian sword, a worldwide movement is beginning to grow, its adherents known as Survivalists. Its devotees train with great intent at being the ones that will survive a nuclear holocaust. Although paramilitary in appearance, these private clubs and organizations have examined in great detail the lifestyle of the ancient ninja warriors, whom they consider to be the ultimate survivalists. Consequently, ninja training methods are being studied and extended to fit their activities. Because of the obvious problems that a nuclear disaster would bring, such as the breakdown of law and order, roving bands of robbers would comb the countryside pillaging in an effort to stay alive. The survivalists maintain that for themselves and their families to manage under such circumstances, personal defence will take priority.

Right and below: *The world survivalist movements have dipped freely into the skills and techniques of the ninja warrior of the past in order to train their members in the skills of survival. The ancient ninja have often been termed the 'ultimate survivalists' and were capable of surmounting extreme weather conditions.*

Right and below: *Frank Dux of the USA about to leap from a cliff top into the sea. In his black garb he approaches the shore taking great care not to be seen, the protruding sea rocks making a perfect camouflage.*

The three levels of thought

Ninja theories can also teach survival in everyday life. The ninja concept is to approach survival in life at three levels, the first level being actual outdoor survival in such circumstances as a car breakdown miles from anywhere, or a person being lost in the wilds far from civilization. Most countries in the winter months in the western hemisphere experience drastic weather conditions and it is not unknown for drivers to be found frozen to death in their cars. A little knowledge of how to stay calm, keep warm and dry, what herbs and plants give sustenance, can make all the difference between living and dying. The art of ninjutsu teaches what to do and how to cope in such situations: ultimately to make you a survivor rather than a statistic. Being a survivor means coping with a given situation when all hope has gone, so the ninja arts extend beyond their martial possibilities.

At the second level of thought, ninja training teaches the adept a way of survival thinking. If you can plan ahead to take care of danger before it arises, then you don't have to worry about it if it ever happens. In simple terms, the long length of nylon cord in the boot of your car, perhaps an extra blanket, maybe even some tinned or dried food packs – even an emergency first-aid kit – will make all the difference. You are ready for the unexpected and will be able to cope. All this creates a more organized life: being prepared without getting too paranoid about it.

The third level of ninja survival training hits out at the very heart of daily life. The conscious sense of awareness spills over from the first two levels and creates a pattern to help you run your own life. The student begins to conduct a well-ordered and prepared life, the first two levels becoming symbols of the third. The student learns that he does not have to waste his energy with negative thoughts and attitudes, when they arise. If you wait to the last minute to do everything, and always in a panic, then how are you going to accomplish anything if you are always worrying about incidentals?

This is not to say that the problems we may face in life should be just brushed under the carpet or forgotten about. In life, we may all have a major problem to face. But by preparing for the eventuality, just like the rations in the car boot in a wintertime breakdown, we can lose the negative aspects by focusing and channelling all our energies directly at the major problem and not wasting them by handling those things which should have been foreseen.

*The father of American ninjutsu, Stephen K. Hayes, adopts the almost hypnotic pose of energy channelling known as **kuji-kiri**. This finger-knitting is part meditative and part psychological, enabling the user to channel his innermost thoughts into one direct endeavour in order to complete successfully the task that lies in front of him.*

Stephen Hayes brings ninjutsu into the modern era by demonstrating a self-defence technique against a gun. In ninjutsu no matter what the weapon used, there is always an answer to it. With subtle taijutsu manoeuvres Hayes manages to turn the tables on his attacker.

The power within

Modern ninjutsu encompasses all these practical and psychological aspects and programmes them into its training curriculum. It could even be said that there is a fourth level of survival, which teaches the student that he has the power within himself to overcome fears. He learns that by building up personal objectives without setting higher limits, he can create within his mind a feeling of success, an air of positivity about his life. Once he has successfully made this step, the momentum it creates gradually begins to develop into a positive attitude and a mental awareness of situations.

Just knowing his capabilities – that he can overcome limits and create successes out of what, to other people, are terrifying conditions – ultimately leads the ninja adept to overcome the unknown fear of his mind. Then all is possible. It is this level of training that takes ninjutsu to its higher order of ideals and enlightenment.

The test of truth

Much of the development of modern ninjutsu in the West has been due mainly to the efforts of three men: Andrew Adams, an American martial arts journalist, whose book *The Invisible Assassins* whetted the appetites of the masses for the ninja and their secret art; Stephen Hayes, the first American ninja who introduced the art to the USA and then to the rest of the world; and the unsung hero of this group, who in true ninja style seemed to want to remain in the shadows, an Israeli called Doron Novon.

It was Novon who first went to Japan to train under Dr Hatsumi personally, and who became the highest-graded Westerner in the arts of ninjutsu. When after many years training he took his fifth *dan* (black belt level of training) he had to undergo more than just a simple test of training competency. Being a fifth *dan* meant that he had reached a higher order of the *ninpo* (spiritual training) ladder and had to pass what was termed 'The Test of Truth'. The first non-Japanese to take this ultimate test of the Togakure ninjutsu system, he sat cross-legged with his back to grandmaster Hatsumi. The master raised his sword above his head, and then, suddenly, struck at the head of Doron Novon. In times gone by, a real sword was used. Today, however, a *bokken* or wooden sword is used, but the blow, if felt, whilst not so final, is still an extremely painful experience. Only a split second separates the student and the deadly blow. If the student can feel or sense the sword coming down and escape, he passes the test. If he fails . . .

Until that day, only five of Hatsumi *sensei's* students had passed the test on their first attempt. In a hushed silence in front of all the other ninja masters Doron Novon took the test. Without any prior warning Hatsumi struck, with not even a change of breath to indicate his movement. The heavy hardwood sword moved at lightning speed towards the skull of the seated Israeli. Within the wink of an eye, it was as if someone, or some unseen force or saviour, had pulled Novon aside. The wooden sword merely sliced through the air and down to the floor, making no contact with anything but the bamboo matting. Novon had passed The Test of Truth and made history at the same time. Such is the power of the mind at the higher levels of training in the art of ninjutsu.

The legend lives on

For all its traditions of secrecy over the many centuries, ninjutsu is still very much alive and in the hands of martial artists who constantly train to attain higher ideals and standards of experiencing life to the full. But one may often wonder in this competitive world of ours, when industrial secrets go missing, or a seized political hostage is suddenly and mysteriously released, if one of the modern-day shadow warriors of the night has been responsible . . .

*A lone ninja armed with a **bo** staff guards the shores of his master's lands. Because the ninja were trained to look for and expect the unexpected at all times, it would seem that the ideal sentry would be a ninja warrior.*

GLOSSARY

B

Bisento
Spear-like weapon with a blade resembling a scimitar fixed to its end; much favoured by the ninja.

Bo
6 ft (1.8 m) wooden staff, around which is built a complete fighting system, and which can be likened to the old English quarterstaff.

Buddhism
Religious doctrine founded in India by the philosopher Gautama (Buddha). In ancient times it was closely connected to the practice of kung-fu, through the Buddhist monks who helped develop the art.

Budo
Warrior way.

Bujinkan
Ninja training hall or club *dojo*. Also the name for Masaaki Hatsumi's organization.

C

Caltrops
Sharp metal spiked weapon for throwing in the pathway of pursuers. Often the tips were poisoned. Natural caltrops used were the spiked shells of the water chestnut fruit. Also known as *tetsubishi*.

Chiba prefecture
Home of Dr Masaaki Hatsumi, the present grandmaster of the Tokagure ninjutsu system.

Chunin
Literally means 'middle person'. The second of the three military ranks in the ninja hierarchy. The *chunin* set the mission for the field ninja to carry out, and was ultimately responsible for its success.

Commando
British army raiding unit raised in World War II by Admiral Sir Roger Keyes. They, like many other elite paramilitary units, have been likened to the ninja of Japan because of their intensive training methods and *modus operandi*.

D

Daikon
Giant Japanese white radish which grows abundantly and has great food value.

Daimyo
Japanese feudal lords.

Dan
Japanese for degree, denoting rank of black belt.

Dojo
The 'place of the way' – a training hall or gymnasium where martial arts are practised.

E

En-no-Gyoja
Yamabushi or mountain warrior ascetic who tried to restore order in Japan in the 6th century by propagating a new way of Buddhism which was called Shugendo.

F

Fu
Ninja method of acting like the 'wind'. Fu is a method of fighting in the ninja body art of taijutsu and is characterized by harmonious interaction with other elements. It gives the user of the *fu* approach the appearance of being everywhere at the same time.

Fudo ken
Ninja clenched fist used for punching and striking body targets.

Fukiya
Pins and poisoned darts shot through a blow-gun at an unsuspecting enemy. Greatly used by many of the ninja clans during stealth activities.

G

Genin
Japanese for 'low person'. A *genin* was a ninja of the lowest rank and the one responsible for actually carrying out the mission. Also called a ninja, although ninja was the collective term for all three levels in the ninja hierarchy.

Globefish
Known also as the blowfish or *fugu*. Its deadly poison was used by the ninja to tip darts and spikes for a faster and more effective kill.

Goton-po
Ninja's five principles of evasion, involving camouflage techniques and concealment tricks by blending in with the natural surroundings of the environment.

Green belt
Standard colour of belt used mostly in the grading examination of ninjutsu to differentiate the novices from the teachers.

H

Hanbo
Ninja 3 ft (1 m) staff or stick, *han* meaning half, and *bo* meaning staff. This weapon is used prolifically in modern ninjutsu training.

Hatsumi
Dr Masaaki Hatsumi, the present leader and 34th grandmaster of the Tokagure ninja.

Hanzo Hattori
Clan chief of the Iga ninja in feudal Japan. Was responsible for the early founding of the Japanese secret service.

Heiho
Study of military strategy; one of the training skills a ninja had to master.

Hombu
Headquarters. This term can be used to define any headquarters for a martial arts school. It is the head or main training place of a martial arts system.

I

Iga
Remote area in feudal Japan where the ninja lived and trained. It is situated on the main island of Honshu.

J

Jonin
Ninja leader who negotiated with the feudal lords over ninja missions and fees exacted.

K

Ka
Ninja fire posture.

Kaginawa
Ninja weapon consisting of a rope with a huge hook on the end for scaling walls and also for entangling a sword-wielding enemy.

Kamar
General term for a fighting posture.

Kantokusha
Male commander of *kunoichi* (female ninja).

Koga
Province in Japan that supported many ninja clans.

Koppo
Bone-breaking techniques of ninjutsu.

Kuji-kiri
Mystical finger-knitting patterns of the ninja. *Kuji* means the number nine. The ninja used this method to channel energy to conjure up their intrinsic powers. Also known as *kuji-in*.

Kunoichi
Female ninja agent.

Kusarifundo
Short weighted chain – a ninja ensnarement weapon.

Kusarigama
Chain and sickle weapon of the ninja.

Kyoketsu shoge
Early ninja weapon consisting of a length of cord with a metal ring attached to one end and a pointed implement such as a knife attached to the other.

M

Mikkyo
Secret doctrines of Shugendo Buddhism. These teachings are said to have originated in Tibet.

Metsubushi
Ninja blinding powder, often thrown at opponents to distract and blind them.

Momochi
Sandayu Momochi, ninja clan leader and teacher of Goemon Ishikawa, the famous bandit hero of Japan.

N

Naginata
Spear-like weapon with a curved blade. First used by infantrymen on the battlefield and later favoured in a shortened staff version by the wives of the samurai warriors.

Ninja
Collective term for the three levels of *genin*, *chunin* and *jonin*. Also known as *shinobi*. One who practises the art of ninjutsu.

Ninja-to (or *ninja-ken*)
Ninja sword. Its straight-edged blade was much shorter than that employed by the samurai.

Ninpo
Higher order of ninjutsu.

O

Oda Nobunaga
Japanese shogun who was the avowed enemy of all ninja. His troops lost the battle of Tensho Iga no Ran in 1579 against the massed ninja clans.

Omyodo
Ancient science, thought to be of Chinese origin, which includes the arts of divination and astrology.

Onshinjutsu
Ninja art of invisibility.

R

Ryu
Japanese for school or style.

S

Saminjutsu
Ninja's art of hypnotism.

Samurai
'One who serves'. The knightly warriors of feudal Japan.

Shuko
Metal band that slipped over the hand, concealing four sharp spikes on the palm side. They were used in pairs for scaling castle walls and other difficult heights. Used as a defence and attack weapon against the sword, the metal spikes would rake the face of an attacker.

Shuriken
Multi-pointed throwing stars used as weapons by ninja agents. These stars, which came in all shapes and sizes, often had the ends tipped in poison. They were carried concealed in a ninja's uniform. Also known as *shaken*.

Shadows of Iga
Ninja appreciation and training society founded by American ninja practitioner Stephen Hayes.

Shinobi
Original name by which the ninja were known.

Shinobishozuki
Ninja uniform. The ninja outfit was usually reversible and had many concealed pockets.

Shinobi-zue
Ninja staff which held a length of chain inside with a heavy weighted end.

Shinto
Indigenous animistic religion of Japan. The word means 'divine spirit way'.

Shogun
Japanese military dictator.

Sojutsu
Ninja spear art.

Sun Tsu
Chinese military genius who wrote a treatise on warfare called *The Art of War*. The ninja clans are said to have arisen from the teachings of this book. Even today it is widely read.

T

Tabi
Ninja split-toed shoe or heavy sock.

Taijutsu
Grappling or body art of ninjutsu. All ninjutsu practised today consists of 90 per cent taijutsu and is the mainstay of the style.

Tanto
Short dirk or dagger of Japanese weaponry.

Tekagi
Similar to the *shuko* but only worn on the legs. Used in pairs this instrument was useful as an aid for climbing walls, trees, etc.

Tetsubishi
See Caltrops.

Tofu
Soft beancurd made from soya beans. Standard ration for the field ninja when out on a mission.

Tokugawa Ieyasu
Founder of the Tokugawa shogunate in 1603. His family ruled Japan for 250 years.

Tsuba
Hand guard of a sword. The ninja's *tsuba* was square shaped rather than the customary round or oval shape of the samurai weapon.

Y

Yamabushi
Mountain warrior hermit priests.

Yari
Spear of the Japanese footsoldier.

Yoko Aruki
Special ninja method of walking for stealth. The word means 'sideways walking'.

Yumi
Bow.

Z

Zen
Religious philosophy that claims one can reach *satori* (enlightenment) through strict meditational practices.